THE
THAI WORLD

TEMPLES, TATTOOS
AND OTHER
CULTURAL ENCOUNTERS

John Hoskin

JOHN BEAUFOY PUBLISHING

In Memory
of My Mother

※ ASIA BOOKS

Published and distributed in Thailand by Asia Books Co., Ltd
No. 65/66, 65/70, 7th Floor, Chamnan Phenjati Business Center,
Rama 9 Road, Huaykwang, Bangkok 10320, Thailand
Tel. (66) 2-715-9000; Fax: (66) 2-715-9197
E-mail: information@asiabooks.com; www.asiabooks.com

First published in the United Kingdom in 2012 by John Beaufoy Publishing,
11 Blenheim Court, 316 Woodstock Road, Oxford OX2 7NS, England
www.johnbeaufoy.com

10 9 8 7 6 5 4 3 2 1

ISBN 978-1-906780-66-1

Designed and typeset in Bembo by Bookcraft Ltd, Stroud, Gloucestershire, UK
Cover design by Lisa McCormick
Project management by Rosemary Wilkinson
Printed in India by Replika Press Pvt Ltd.

CONTENTS

INTRODUCTION

I hadn't intended to stay long. Arriving in Bangkok in early 1979 I thought I'd spend a couple of years working and exploring the country and then return to my native England. Three decades later I find myself still here. Why? It's a question all long-time expats are frequently asked, although I've never been able to come up with a truly adequate answer. Perhaps that's not surprising when Bangkok itself is elusive, resisting any easy definition and persisting in a paradoxical mix of the traditional and the modern, of charm and chaos, by turns wondrous and woeful.

It is perhaps in Bangkok's quintessential paradoxes that lie at least one answer as to why I have chosen to stay here so long; it is as a result of the unexpected. And that underscores precisely what the city and Thai culture as a whole are all about – the ability to constantly surprise, to offer fresh encounters.

Thailand and Thai culture are exotic. That may be an adjective reduced to a cliché by travel brochures, where it is usually meant to conjure up images of tropical beaches or gilded temples, but it is truly applicable in the Concise Oxford Dictionary's definition as meaning 'remarkably strange or unusual; bizarre'. In spite of the effects of mass tourism and globalization, Thailand is unusual, indeed exotic, in that it preserves much of its unique traditional culture very largely intact.

These collected articles were originally written to meet the demands of particular magazines and particular editors – to all of whom I am grateful – and as such do not offer a comprehensive account of Thai culture. They do aim, however, to highlight facets of Thai life, aspects that are in most cases readily seen and yet defining in their own way of the 'Thainess' that indelibly stamps the culture of a country and a people so fascinating and, ultimately, so endearing.

5

THE
BUDDHIST WORLD

Thailand is a strongly Buddhist country, with more than 90% of the population professing and practising Theravada Buddhism, the national religion, supported by some 30,000 Buddhist monasteries throughout the country and a religious community of about 250,000 monks. The faith has become so integrated with Thai society that the two are hardly separable, with Buddhist influences found in virtually all aspects of Thai culture from daily life to art and architecture.

THE THAI TEMPLE

You can't please all of the people all of the time; some people never. Thai temples – *wat* in Thai – are magnificent buildings, testaments to both an enduring faith and to centuries of cultural endeavour. But they are highly distinctive and you need to meet them halfway for a full appreciation. Some people fail to take the correct approach and hence miss the true attraction. English writer Geoffrey Gorer is a case in point.

In his 1936 travel book *Bali and Angkor*, Gorer does not mask his displeasure with Thailand. 'It is very difficult to take Bangkok quite seriously; it is the most hokum place I have ever seen, never having been to California,' he wrote. Prompting his sneers was Thai traditional temple architecture, which he thought 'the same as Cambodian, but with knobs on – lots of knobs.'

It seemed to Gorer that 'wherever a bit of decoration or twirly-whirly can be fixed with some possibility of its staying put it is stuck on.' The elaborate adornment of Bangkok's Wat Arun finally proved too much. Gorer repeats a guidebook suggestion that the temple is best seen from a distance and adds, 'Yes, indeed. You can't be too far away from these buildings to get the best effect.'

On this showing Gorer would clearly have a thing or two to tell St Peter about Heaven's Gate. His criticisms are unfair, however, and he uses a mundane yardstick for assessing what is the truly fabulous. Ironically it was a writer of more famous acerbity, Somerset Maugham, who perceived and accepted the real wonder of the Thai temple. In his book *The Gentleman in the Parlour* (1930) he writes:

7

'They are unlike anything in the world, so that you are taken aback, and you cannot fit them into a scheme of the things you know.' 'It makes you laugh with delight to think that anything so fantastic could exist on this sombre earth. They are gorgeous; they glitter with gold and whitewash, yet are not garish; against that vivid sky, in that dazzling sunlight, they hold their own, defying the brilliancy of nature and supplementing it with the ingenuity and playful boldness of man.'

Maugham captures the delight that nearly all visitors to Thailand find in the country's temples. They are rightly at the top of anyone's sightseeing list. The immediate attractions lie, as Maugham so vividly portrays, in their fabulous appearance, their exotic architecture, their wealth of decorative detail.

Yet there is more than just the initial visual impact; a closer look at Buddhist temples opens up a whole world of understanding about Thai society and its art and culture. Buddhism, along with the tradition of monarchy, underpins the nation's entire cultural and social fabric. It is the religion under which the people (originally animists) were first united and it has remained a vital and visible force in daily life throughout the more than 700 years of Thai history. Today it is as strong as ever, practised and professed by more than nine-tenths of the population.

Quintessential to the religion is the monkhood. Central to Buddhist practice is the concept of making merit and the supreme form of merit, for men at least, is to become, if only temporarily, a monk. Even in modern Thailand most young men will still comply with this custom, becoming ordained and entering a monastery for a period of perhaps one, two or three months.

The concept of merit-making and the various ways in which it may be achieved, as well as the deeper meaning and practice of Buddhism and its attendant monkhood, need not concern us here. What is important to grasp for an appreciation of the Thai temple is the integral role of the religious community and hence the material structure which supports it.

The word 'temple' is largely unsatisfactory as a translation of the Thai word *wat*. It implies a single structure, as is the case with a Christian church, but this is not so with a Buddhist *wat*. Besides monks' residential quarters which are commonly, though not always, found at a *wat*, a Thai temple complex comprises several distinct religious buildings.

The principal structure is the *bot*, the most sacred part of the temple and the place where ordination ceremonies are conducted. The building is identified by eight boundary stones, called *sima*, placed outside at the four corners and the four cardinal points.

A temple will also probably have one or more *viharn*, a hall similar to a *bot* but without the *sima*. This building is used as a sermon hall for monks and lay worshippers. Both the *viharn* and the *bot* enshrine Buddha statues: a presiding image and commonly several smaller attendant statues. Many of these images are of great antiquity and some are individually famous, revered as possessing unusual spiritual powers.

The *bot* and *viharn* follow identical architectural styles, being rectangular buildings with sweeping multi-tiered roofs covered with glazed brown and green or blue tiles. Each end of the roof's peak terminates in a gilded finial known as a *cho fa*, or 'sky tassel'. A gracefully curved ornamentation, it looks like a slender bird's neck and head, and is generally believed to represent the mythical *garuda*, half bird, half man.

Along with the *bot* and *viharn*, the most characteristic of temple structures is the *chedi* or *stupa*. Dominating the compound of a *wat*, this is a tall decorative spire constructed over relics of the Buddha, sacred texts or an image. Essentially there are two basic forms: bell-shaped and raised on square or round terraces of diminishing size, tapering to a thin spire, or a round, finger-like tower. The latter, derived from Khmer architecture and symbolic of the mythical mountain abode of the gods, is known as a *prang*.

Other buildings in a temple compound can include a library for sacred texts and a *mondop*. Traditionally the former was built on stilts over a pond to protect the fragile manuscripts from white ants. The *mondop* is a square-shaped building with tapering roof enshrining some relic, often a Buddha footprint, a decorated stone impression far larger than lifesize. These, like the *chedi*, are not merely architectural features, they also serve as monuments in the true sense, objects to instruct and focus the mind.

Some larger *wats* may also have cloisters, open-sided galleries perhaps displaying rows of Buddha images, while bell towers and various pavilions can be additional features.

Generally, *wats* further have a crematorium, identified by its needle-like chimney and, usually, a school for monks and perhaps also for lay children. These buildings are indicative of one of the traditional functions of a temple which extended beyond those of a place of worship and home to a religious community. Rather like a medieval Christian church, the Thai temple was the focal point of every village. Unlike the church, however, it served far more than the community's spiritual needs. In the past, and still today in some rural areas, cultural life revolved around the *wat* which stood as social services centre, school, hospital, dispensary, hostelry and village news, employment and information agency.

The most vivid illustration of the *wat's* community role and social focal point these days is the annual temple fair. Most *wats* continue the tradition of what are essentially fund-raising events but also occasions for *sanuk*, having fun. At these times the normally quiet temple compound becomes filled with swings and round-abouts, sideshows, *likay* (folk opera) theatre shows and all the other typical fun-of-the-fair amusements, while the otherwise serene air is rent by loudspeakers blaring out raucous Thai music.

In a more serious vein, the temple has also been the store-house of knowledge, sacred and secular (as with herbal medicine, for example) and monks, as one commentator has put it, 'provided the vasty majority of the inhabitants of pre-modern Siam with the ultimate basis for making sense of the world.'

Thailand's high literacy rate, both now and in the past, owes much to temple schools where youngsters are taught to read the sacred texts. On the day-to-day practical level abbots will also often take the lead in instigating community projects, such as digging a village well.

Most fascinating from the visitor's point of view is the temple as art centre. Unlike the *wat's* other functions, this role was unwittingly assumed. Until the modern period all Thai art was religious art, it had no conscious aesthetic function and served purely didactic and devotional purposes. Thus sculpture, painting and the minor arts, for example, gilt-on-lacquer, mother-of-pearl inlay and woodcarving, found expression almost exclusively in temple decoration.

Sculpture was largely limited to images of the Buddha, while classical painting achieved its finest expression in murals. Typically these were painted on all four walls of *bots* and *viharns*, though, due to the fragile nature of the medium and the ravages of the climate, few surviving examples pre-date the 18th century.

All murals were purely didactic in purpose and the classic formula was to decorate the side walls with episodes from the life of the Buddha or his previous incarnations, individual scenes being sepa-rated by registers of praying celestial beings. The back wall generally showed a graphic interpretation of the Buddhist cosmology and the front wall was covered with the scene of Buddha's victory over Mara (a force of evil and temptation).

Typically murals lack any attempt at perspective and figures tend to be small, while the entire picture area is 'busy' and filled with detail. Because of the latter convention, artists often completed back-grounds with genre scenes of Thai daily life. These are fascinating both for their content and as areas where the painters display greater self-expression.

Doors and window shutters also sometimes have painted scenes, while all flat surfaces are commonly brilliantly adorned. Especially notable among the decorative arts are mother-of-pearl inlay and gilt-on-lacquer work which frequently have a high pictorial quality. Coloured glass mosaic is also quite often used and adds to a temple's lavish overall decoration. Brilliant and kaleidoscopic, such adornment is effective, strangely managing to avoid the garish and not distract from the overall ambience of quiet devotion.

In many and varied ways the temple affords fascinating scope for approaching and appreciating the very heart of Thai culture. As for Geoffrey Gorer's 'knobs' and 'twirly-whirly' bits, well, he obviously had no sense of joy, of that natural exuberance which itself is quintessentially Thai.

SACRED IMAGES

Nowhere else in the world possesses more Buddha statues than Thailand. Buddhism has been the faith of the people since the 13th-century birth of the Kingdom and the essence of the religion, its teachings and the focus of its practice, is centred on the image of the Buddha. Sacred images are encountered everywhere, in homes, from royal palaces to the humblest of village dwellings, in offices, in shops, at wayside shrines and, of course, in the country's ubiquitous Buddhist temples.

The distinction of the Buddha image, however, is one of more than just quantity – scarcely any other religious icon is as intriguing in its form, function and the variety of its depiction, as well as in what can seem to foreigners certain paradoxes. Contrary to some foreign perceptions, the Buddha image is not an idol in the sense of being an object of worship. You will see devotees kneeling before a statue as they make offerings but the image properly serves as a reminder of the Buddha's teachings, and it is to those that, strictly speaking, worshippers pay their respects.

The aesthetics of the Buddha image are more truly a paradox. Just as they are not idols, they are neither perceived nor conceived as works of art and their creation is an act of devotion and of merit-making, not of self-expression. And yet numerous statues undoubtedly possess great beauty, and Buddha sculpture in general ranks among Thailand's highest artistic achievements. There is no simple explanation for this other than that the extraordinary skill of Thai sculptors and bronze casters has always found full expression – especially in form, line and depiction of serenity – through devotion to the creation of a sacred image. An image-maker did not consciously seek originality and when, inevitably, it did occur it was in spite of, or secondary to his conscious aims.

While there is great and original artistic beauty in many Thai Buddha statues, every image is supposed to be a faithful copy, theoretically adhering to a convention built up from descriptions recorded during the Buddha's lifetime, although, in accordance with his express wish, no likenesses were made until long after his death. Even then, once images were fashioned, artists saw themselves as essentially copyists, keeping to strict guidelines and reproducing certain features that were accepted as integral.

Firstly, the Buddha, as the Great Teacher, is represented as a human being and likenesses display none of the fantastic anatomy of, say, the multi-armed, four-headed forms of certain Hindu gods. And yet the Enlightened One is understood as a remarkable personage, bearing 32 major and 80 minor marks which distinguished him from other mortals. Not all of these – the sound of his voice, for instance – lend themselves to visual representation but a few were established as hallmarks of all Buddha sculptures. Especially characteristic are the *ushnisha* or cranial protuberance, hair curling in a clockwise direction and extended ear lobes.

Aside from these underlying conventions, several other factors account for the considerable variety to be found in Thai Buddha images. Most obvious are the wide range of materials used and the size of a sculpture. A statue may be only a few centimetres tall, while others reach several metres. The reclining figure at Bangkok's Wat Po, for example, measures 46 metres (150 feet). As for materials, images have been carved in virtually every suitable substance, from wood to rock crystal, but most especially have been cast in bronze, casting being a skill in which the Thais have always been extremely adept.

More specific to religious expression, Buddha images differ in three fundamental ways – in form or pose, in gestures expressed and in sculptural style.

In form, images are confined to just four possible postures: standing, seated, reclining and walking, the first two being the most popular with Thai sculptors. The standing pose, with legs straight and the feet parallel, does not vary, other than in the folds of the robe, which may be shown in the covered mode, with both shoulders clothed, or 'open', leaving the right shoulder exposed. In the seated posture, however, there are three different ways in which the legs may be placed: the 'hero' posture (*virasana*), with the legs folded, one lying on top of the other; the 'adamantine' posture (*vajrasana*), where the legs are crossed in such a way that each foot rests on the opposite thigh with the soles turned upwards and the 'European' posture (*pralambanasana*), which is the ordinary position of someone seated in a chair.

The reclining pose shows the Buddha lying on his side with the right hand supporting the head and represents the moment of the Enlightened One's passing and entering Nirvana. The last of the four postures, walking, was an innovation of Thai sculptures, who were the first to cast the figure in the round, whereas previously it had been sculpted only in relief. In a supremely graceful pose, the Buddha is shown in a frozen step, one foot firmly planted on the ground, the other with the heel lifted; one arm is raised with the palm of the hand forward, while the other swings naturally at the side of the body. The pose, which is comparatively rare, was inspired by the story of the Buddha's descending from heaven after preaching to his mother.

With the exception of the reclining figure, which is unchanging, the postures of the Buddha image are further differentiated by the depiction of hand gestures (*mudras*) that recall various events in his lifetime. In the iconography these are numerous and sometimes recondite, although only half a dozen are commonly portrayed.

Seated and standing figures are by far the most frequently encountered and it is these which display the *mudras* most popular with Thai

15

sculptors. In the seated pose, the two most common gestures found are 'meditation' (*samadhi*), with both hands lying in the lap palm upwards, and 'calling the Earth to witness' (*bhumisparsa*), also know as 'victory over Mara' (*maravijaya*), Mara being a force of evil and temptation. The pose is similar to 'meditation' except that the right hand rests on the right knee with the fingers pointed downwards.

Much less common in the seated image, although still one of the principal *mudras*, is 'setting the wheel of law in motion' (*dharmacakra*), in which the two hands are held in front of the chest, the fingertips of the left touching the palm of the right hand.

The most often seen *mudras* for standing and walking figures are 'dispelling fear' (*abhaya*), in which the right hand (occasionally both hands) is held palm forward with fingers upward, and 'exposition' or 'giving instruction' (*vitarka*), a similar gesture but with the right forefinger and thumb touching. The last of the six main *mudras*, usually reserved for the standing image, is 'charity' (*varada*), also referred to as 'choice' or 'the object chosen' (*vara*), where the right arm is hanging with the open palm facing outward and the fingers pointing straight down.

All principal Buddhist iconography is rooted primarily in Indian sculpture and initially received in what is now Thailand via the major pre-Thai civilizations, particularly those of the Mon, the Khmer and the southern power of Srivijaya. Styles of sculpture, however, have evolved considerably over the centuries and, while influenced by their cultural predecessors, the Thais developed their own distinctive sculptural schools, beginning with the founding of their first sovereign capital at Sukhothai in the 13th century.

It was here that Thai art had its first and arguably finest flowering, the most beautiful and most original Buddha images dating from this period. The images produced were far more stylized than anything that had gone before, being marked by a greater fluidity in the line of the body and an uncanny degree of serenity and spirituality expressed in the facial features.

Principal characteristics are a tall flame halo, small hair curls, oval face, arched eyebrows, hooked nose and a smiling expression. In addition, the artists tended to emphasize supernatural features such as the cranial protuberance, extended earlobes, long arms and flat-soled feet with projecting heels. Statues in the seated posture were popular but the real triumph of the Sukhothai artists, and perhaps the highest artistic achievement in Thai sculpture, was the walking Buddha.

At roughly the same time as Sukhothai was establishing itself, the Thais in the north of the country were united in the Lanna kingdom which had its capital at Chiang Mai, founded in 1296. Its school of art is generally referred to as Chiang Saen style, named after the town which was an early power base of the region and where a number of images of great merit have been found.

Chiang Saen art falls into two basic groups, early and late. The images of the former exemplify Indian Pala styles which were probably inherited from Haripunchai (present-day Lamphun), an offshoot of the Mon Dvaravati kingdom which was conquered by Lanna. Distinctive characteristics are a halo in the form of a lotus bud, round face, prominent chin and a stout body with a well-developed chest.

The later period, at its height during the reign of the Lanna King Tilokaraja (1442–87), coincided with the blossoming of Theravada Buddhism in the north and shows both Sukhothai and Sri Lankan influences in the flame halo, oval face and more slender body of the Buddha images. In art as well as politics, both Lanna and Sukhothai eventually became subordinate to Ayutthaya, a younger Thai kingdom centred on the Chao Phraya river basin. The sculpture of this period falls into two categories, that of U-Thong or early Ayutthaya (12–15th centuries) and Ayutthaya proper which lasted until the mid-18th century.

U-Thong images passed through stages during which Dvaravati, Khmer and Sukhothai styles in turn dominated, though they are essentially typified by a square face and a stern expression.

In the Ayutthaya style proper the heritage of Sukhothai came to outweigh that of the Khmer but the U-Thong form never completely vanished and the Buddha images of this period are scarcely comparable to the achievements of Sukhothai's Golden Age. Considerable distinction was achieved, however, in the late Ayutthaya period when Buddhas in royal attire, elaborately adorned with jewellery, were widely produced.

The current period of Thai art, that of Bangkok, dates from the establishment of the present-day capital in 1782. Little innovation is apparent in the Buddhas produced in the 19th century, although one masterpiece does date from the reign of King Rama III (1824–51). This is the giant statue of the reclining Buddha enshrined at Wat Po, which is an extremely serene image in spite of its massive size tending to overpower aesthetic appreciation.

Increasingly in the Bangkok period artists have tended to produce more lifelike images and while the traditional characteristics, such as the flame halo and extended earlobes, are shown, the overall effect is that of a more humanized figure. A fine example of this is the standing Buddha that was made to commemorate the 2,500th anniversary of Buddhism in 1957 and which today is housed in the National Museum at Bangkok.

MONKS AND ORDINATION

A senior Buddhist monk dressed in customary saffron robes ascends on an elevated platform, rising beside THAI's latest aircraft shimmering on the tarmac in the bright tropical sunlight. Religious chants fill the air as the monk rises to the level of the plane's nosecone. He reaches across and inscribes in white paste an ancient Buddhist blessing on what is the most modern of high-tech aviation equipment. A sprinkling of lustral water concludes the ceremony, one held sacred in Thai culture long before man ever learnt to fly.

It's an odd, arresting scene that takes place every time Thailand's national carrier inaugurates a new aircraft. Few people witness it, if only because it usually takes place early in the morning at a time officially pronounced auspicious. Yet the ceremony encapsulates the enduring role of Buddhism and the monkhood.

Throughout the kingdom's 700-year history the national religion has been a constant thread running through the cultural fabric, providing a common bond and giving crucial definition to the society. Today, the spirit of the religion remains as strong as ever. The lasting impact of this cohesive force is readily apparent and pervades the entire country. Skylines are characterized by the gilded spires of awe-inspiring Buddhist temples, while files of saffron-robed monks on morning alms rounds are recurring images at the start of the day in cities, towns and villages.

Fundamental to Buddhism is the monkhood which serves the laity as well as its own individual goals. Most young men, as noted in the chapter on the Thai temple, will become a monk if only temporarily, to make merit. For women and the population in general, important merit is made in the practice of giving daily food offerings to monks.

In addition to serving merit-making ends, monks also actively participate in society. Not only do they preside over temple rituals, they further conduct important ceremonies in the community at large. These typically include the blessing of new homes, offices or business ventures.

With the monastic system playing such a crucial role, present-day Thailand supports a religious community of some 250,000 monks who reside at an estimated 30,000 temples throughout the country.

There is, naturally, a permanent religious community but the majority of Thailand's monks are ordained for only a short spell. It may be just a few days but the usual practice is to remain in a monastery throughout one *Phansa*, the three-month Rains Retreat. Sometimes misleadingly referred to as Buddhist Lent, this period runs from July to October, its precise dates following the lunar calendar.

The reason for becoming a monk is the same as it always has been and is basically two-fold. In being ordained a young man earns merit for his parents. For himself, a monk furthers his progress towards Nirvana (release from all suffering and the cycle of death and rebirth which is the ultimate goal of Buddhism) by a deeper understanding of the Buddha's teachings gained through study, self-deprivation and meditation.

To be ordained into the Buddhist monkhood, even temporarily, means cutting all ties with mundane life. A monk-to-be, for example, must have no worldly obligations, such as outstanding debts. As for quitting one's job, so accepted is the practice of becoming a monk in Thailand that government agencies and private companies all have provision for 'ordination leave' in their terms of employment.

Once decided on becoming a monk, the candidate will be given a date for his ordination by the abbot of the temple he is

to enter. In the meantime he should pay visits to all his acquain-
tances, announcing the news and begging their forgiveness for any
misdeeds. This clears away temporal ties, loose ends, as it were, in
human relationships.

At this time, the candidate is known as *chao nak*, literally 'dragon',
a reference to a Buddhist myth in which a dragon sought to become
a monk. On the eve of the ordination a lay ceremony is held, usually
at home, during which the monk-to-be has his head and eyebrows
ritually shaved. The first few locks are generally cut off by his parents
and other family members, while the job is completed by an experienced hand. The shaving of head and eyebrows is a symbolic denial
of vanity and sexuality. At this stage, a transitional phase between
layman and monk, the candidate is believed to be especially vulner-
able to accidents and it is probable that the title *chao nak* is used to
confuse the spirits which could cause harm. This would be similar to
the belief in the protective power of nicknames or to the custom of
changing names if a child becomes seriously ill.

Once shaved, the monk-to-be is dressed in white robes and
becomes the focus of the *Tham Kwan Nak* ceremony, conducted not
by monks but by a professional expert in such affairs. For anywhere
up to two or three hours this master of ceremonies recites verses that
recount essentially the suffering of the candidate's mother in giving
birth and the hardships endured by the parents in raising their child.
The ceremony is usually concluded with feasting and entertainment
in which the candidate will take part, his last such indulgence before
the accepting the austere lifestyle of a monk.

On the day of his ordination the candidate, in white robes, is
carried on the shoulders of friends to the temple. Again this probably
parallels the event in the Buddha's life when, as Prince Siddhattha,
he rode away from his father's palace on horseback. On reaching its
destination, the joyous and lively procession circumambulates the
temple's main sanctuary three times. At the same time the *chao nak*
scatters coins in a symbolic gesture of rejecting material possessions.

The candidate's father, carrying a saffron robe, leads his son into the temple where the monks are assembled. Accepting the robe from his father, the *chao nak* kneels in front of the abbot and humbly pays his respects before asking to be ordained. In so doing he undertakes to observe the ten basic vows of a novice monk – five in addition to the five fundamental precepts all Buddhists should follow.

Next an examination takes place during which the abbot questions the candidate as to his fitness to become a monk. He should, for example, testify that he is over 20 years of age (younger novices are accepted in certain ordinations), that he possesses the saffron robe and alms bowl, that he has been given a Buddhist name and has had an instructor in the faith (the latter usually being the abbot presiding at the ceremony).

The results of the investigation are reported to the assembled monks, asking for their acceptance of the candidate into the order. Once accepted he is then helped into the saffron robes. To conclude the ceremony the new monk pours water from a silver container in a symbolic gesture of transferring the merit he makes in becoming a monk to his parents.

All ordination ceremonies follow essentially the same pattern but there are variations in the pre-ordination celebrations. Most spectacular are the few mass ordinations that are traditional to certain local communities, the best known being those held in the small northern town of Mae Hong Son and at Haad Siew near the ancient ruined city of Si Satchanalai. Both involve the ordination of young boys and are culturally distinct in the form but not content of their rituals.

These affairs are firstly distinguished as being communal festivities in which everyone takes part. Held over two or three days, these particular mass ordination ceremonies are noted for their grandeur – the elephant procession at Haad Siew and the gorgeous costumes of the novices-to-be in Mae Hong Son. But while considerable emphasis is placed on the colourful displays, their symbolic meaning is the same as in less spectacular pre-ordination rituals.

All is meant to parallel the historic events in the Buddha's life. Prior to questing and achieving enlightenment the Buddha was the son of the ruler of a small kingdom or city state. As such he lived a life of luxury, material comforts protecting him from the world's sufferings. After he became aware of sickness and death, he left his father's palace and sought through self-denial to find a path that could release man from suffering.

The mass ordination ceremonies of Mae Hong Son and Haad Siew thus highlight the renunciation of material wealth. In the pre-ordination festivities the candidates appear as young princes. When they go to the temple to be accepted either into the priesthood or as novices, they discard the finery, the jewellery, the make-up as a gesture of relinquishing worldly goods and the vanity and desire that accompanies them.

Whether it is a relatively simple affair among family and close friends, or a protracted grand celebration in which a whole community participates, ordination is one of the most important events in the life of Thai men. It is an occasion they will always remember, marking the transition from youth to adult maturity.

After a spell in the monkhood a young man should have a more meaningful understanding of the world and be better prepared to lead a life in accordance with the teachings of the Buddha.

THE BUDDHIST
'RAINS RETREAT'

When you have a monk in the house is the best time to practise Buddhism. That is one logical explanation for the origin of *Phansa*, the traditional Buddhist 'Rains Retreat' as celebrated in Thailand. A three-month period beginning on the first waning of the 8th moon, generally in July, Phansa is the time when Buddhist monks pledge themselves to remain in their monastery. Ordinary folk also pay closer attention to religious practice at this time.

As the theory goes, the Rains Retreat began long ago before the widespread existence of monasteries. At that time, wandering mendicant monks who travelled the country would seek temporary shelter for the duration of the monsoon season. Villagers accordingly provided huts and thus, owing to the presence of the monks, people came to view the rainy months as the season most appropriate to the exercise of religion.

A different account of the origins of Phansa, dating back to the religion's earliest days when the Buddha was still alive, reflects the lay population in a more irritable mood. The rainy season, when the ground is soft and muddy, is the time for planting rice and, so the story has it, villagers became annoyed at wandering monks who trod everywhere, inadvertently trampling the seed-lings. Word of this got back to the Buddha and so he made a ruling that monks must stay in their monasteries during the period of the rains.

Whatever the precise origins of the practice, Phansa remains an important event in the Thai Buddhist calendar. It bears some relation to the Christian Lent and not only do monks limit their movements, become more strict in their prayers and give more sermons but the laity also variously restricts its usual pleasures.

As with virtually all religious festivals in Thailand, *Phansa* is typified by colourful joyous celebrations. These are held to mark the beginning and end of the period recognized throughout the country but variously honoured in different regions, some of which hold more closely to past traditions.

The start of the Rains Retreat – *Khao Phansa* (*khao* literally means 'to enter') – has long been marked by villagers fashioning huge wax candles, as tall or taller than a man, which are taken in procession and presented to the local temple. These candles will then illuminate the temple's presiding Buddha image for the duration of *Phansa*.

As with so much of Thailand's traditional life, the practice of celebrating Khao Phansa is today best witnessed in the north-east, the most intensely rural part of the country where the people still cling tenaciously to time-honoured customs. Here, in the provincial centre of Ubol Ratchathani, the Candle Festival is a major event in the local festive calendar.

Today groomed as a lively tourist attraction, the festival is a dazzling affair featuring parades through the city streets of huge, beautifully carved, beeswax candles. Some stand several metres tall and all are adorned from top to bottom with intricate designs. The floats on which they are paraded are similarly ornate, featuring mythical creatures and other Thai motifs. Competitions are held for the best creations, and overall the occasion is one of joy, colour and festive fun.

The essential meaning of it all, however, is not forgotten and after being exhibited the candles are presented to temples where they serve their true purpose. The festival thus wonderfully combines a showcase of the people's artistry as well as a display of their piety.

The celebration of *Khao Phansa*, as with so many other religious festivities, is closely linked to the agricultural cycle. It is the season when the back-breaking task of planting out the young rice seedlings has been completed. The moment thus creates a natural pause in the farming calendar, a moment to relish a welcome break from work in the fields.

Yet a lull in the crucial activity of rice cultivation is not all feasting and fun. Momentarily freed from agricultural labour, young men have the opportunity to enter the monkhood for a short spell.

For the lay community at large, Phansa is generally a period for greater displays of piety. People go to the temple more frequently to listen to sermons and they give offerings to the monks as it has been traditionally thought more merit is to be earned when such acts are performed during the Rains Retreat.

The custom of presenting gifts culminates at the end of the period, *Ok Phansa* (*ok* literally means 'coming out') which marks the beginning of *Thod Krathin* when the people offer new robes to the monastic community. It is an elaborate affair involving considerable ceremonial, with processions and displays of the gifts.

Thod Krathin takes place throughout the country, though it was traditionally most spectacularly celebrated in the capital where the King would travel with much pomp and pageantry by royal barge to a riverside temple and there make the customary offering of new robes.

A reflection of the waterborne celebration of Thod Krathin is found in the northern town of Nan which marks the festival with boat races. At this time the otherwise sleepy Nan river comes alive as sleek, brightly painted wooden longboats, paddled by scores of rowers, compete for the honours in races between local teams. All the fun of the fair accompanies the event and the river banks are crammed with spectators, food stalls, sideshows and amusements.

As religious festivals closely parallel the agricultural cycle and may well have their roots in ancient animistic practices, water features large in the celebration of *Ok Phansa*. It is the end of Lent but it is also the end of the monsoon season when country folk express gratitude for the months of live-giving rains on which the annual rice crop depends.

Thus rivers are natural focal points for festivities. The most captivating of such celebrations is the 'Illuminated Boat Procession' held on the Mekong at Nakhon Phanom, in the north-east. The highlight of the event is a flotilla on the river of scores of boats lit up with hundreds of flickering oil lamps deftly arranged to delineate palaces and other enchanting pictures in light.

Varied though *Ok Phansa* festivities are, and however allied they may be to observances rooted in the agricultural cycle, Buddhism provides the celebrations with a religious core. Most emphatically the end of the Rains Retreat honours an important event in the life of the Buddha. According to religious belief, the Buddha spent one *Phansa* period preaching to his mother in heaven. Afterwards he returned to earth, descending a crystal ladder, flanked by gold and silver ladders on which followed the gods Indra and Brahma. At the moment of descent, the Buddha performed the miracle of 'opening all the worlds to view', whereby the various levels of heaven and hell and all the continents were laid bare and equidistant to the eyes.

The occasion is today honoured at the Tak Bat Devo festival in Uthai Thani. Held the day following *Ok Phansa*, it features a procession of monks descending from a hilltop temple to receive offerings from the people.

Remembrance of the time the Buddha spent preaching in heaven not only adds distinction to the celebration of *Ok Phansa*, it has also had a significant impact on religious art. The Buddha's descent inspired the iconography of the 'Walking Buddha' image, while pictorial representation of the event provided tremendous scope for mural artists.

A monk sheltering from the rains may in the past have prompted greater religious observance. Today, for the visitor to Thailand, consideration of the annual Rains Retreat affords an ideal opportunity for witnessing traditional celebrations that are echoed in the life and art of the nation.

THE SUPERNATURAL WORLD

However modern a culture appears on the surface, it will have a hidden, sometimes darker side. Thailand is no different. A transcendental realm of little-understood phenomena – of spirits and demons, of demands for propitiation, of forces of good and evil – is surprisingly influential in the everyday life of the Thais.

SPIRITUAL TATTOOS

The room is eerily quiet, the silence deepened by a sense of awe provoked as much by the sight of a dozen tough young men sitting solemnly on the floor as by the array of religious symbols.

The scene is all the more striking for being so unexpected. The outside of the house seems like any other in this anonymous Bangkok suburb. Raised on concrete posts, it is a common modern variation of a traditional Thai home, neither rich nor poor. Nothing disturbs the peace of a quiet Sunday afternoon and you might imagine a family resting after the midday meal.

Not so. The master of the house is very much at work. In that large, hushed room he cuts an imposing figure. Dressed in robes and wearing a gilded mask, he perches cross-legged on a throne draped around with flower garlands and quasi-religious trappings, and could almost be mistaken for some outlandish native chieftain with his youthful warriors kneeling at his feet like subjects paying homage.

In reality no petty potentate, the masked figure nonetheless commands enormous respect from those who visit him. As a renowned tattooist he has a wide following and the young men waiting patiently on this Sunday afternoon have all come to add to their already impressive collections of body art.

It is art in a way and the tattooist displays great dexterity as he prods rapidly with a steel needle, pricking out in blue ink finely drawn classical figures and words of arcane writing on the backs, chests, arms, legs, even necks of his clients.

The practice of marking the skin to a greater or lesser extent with tattoos has been widespread among the Thais for centuries. Its beginnings are obscure, though it is possible that the custom reached Thailand via the ancient Khmer, who were a powerful presence in the region prior to the 13th-century birth of the Thai nation. Certainly, it is known from the evidence of early European travellers that tattoos were common in Thailand by at least the 16th century. Old temple murals also suggest body markings were popular in the Ayutthaya period. Paintings in the northern town of Nan, for example, portray soldiers wearing tattoos to protect them in battle.

In spite of acquiring something of a social stigma in modern times, tattoos have remained popular among certain groups of, usually, young men. Tattoos may also be invisible, incised with clear sesame oil, and so even if body markings are frowned upon by some people, it is not necessarily only labourers and other toughs who go through the process: men in all walks of life (very few women choose to be tattooed) may have 'hidden' tattoos.

Invisible tattoos perhaps seem to defeat the object of the exercise – why have them if they cannot be seen and admired? Well, Thai tattooing is less cosmetic and more supernatural.

Unlike the Western male's preference for naked women, dagger-pierced hearts, eagles and other standard patterns from the tattooist's catalogue, the Thais opt for more arcane symbols – mythical creatures, magical spells and cabalistic diagrams. The difference is not merely one of aesthetic taste; it illustrates a fundamental distinction. Tattoos in Thailand are, in a word, magic. Spiritual tattoos, as they may be termed, are supernatural in that they serve the implicit purpose of providing protection from and power over external forces. It is something deeply rooted in spiritual life.

Although the majority of the Thai population is Buddhist, not only professing but also practising the religion, the faith does not address mundane problems. Buddhism is concerned with man's ultimate release from suffering, from the cycle of death and rebirth. As such it offers little to ward off the threats and dangers, real or perceived, of everyday life. At the same time, the religion is tolerant, not necessarily negating extraneous beliefs. Accordingly, the Thais have inherited from their animistic ancestors a host of beliefs in supernatural powers which interact with ordinary life. These do not contradict Buddhism and, indeed, are held in such a complex relationship with the national religion that an outsider can scarcely differentiate the dual elements.

Vanity may be involved and, as in the West, tattoos can be seen as implying manliness and toughness. In the past, tattoos among certain Thai-Lao groups of northern Thailand, for example, were taken largely as signs of male courage or as tokens to please lovers. In this instance the body was tattooed from the waist to just below the knee. The custom has now largely vanished, however, and it bears only a superficial relation to the widespread and continuing practice of spiritual tattooing.

An element of masculine pride, however, need not be divorced from tattoos that serve a supernatural purpose. This is especially so today when some young men may display a kind of macho vanity and make a cult out of collecting tattoos.

'I think they look good,' said one young man proudly displaying an impressive collection of designs covering his well-muscled torso. But another tattooee (to coin a necessary word), when asked why he had tattoos, replied that he felt they gave him a sense of well-being.

Although vanity may be involved, it is strictly secondary to a belief in a supernatural element. There is a tendency to prefer attractive tattoos but equally there is a tendency to associate attractiveness with supernatural power. The idea of toughness implicit in being tattooed is likewise related to the object not the act – power is intrinsic in the tattoo itself, not in the experience of undergoing the process of tattooing.

The majority of people who are tattooed believe they acquire two types of strength, *kwam yu yong kong kraphan* and *metta mahaniyom*. The first is physical invulnerability from weapons with tattoos preventing the skin from being punctured by knives or bullets. The second is the power to attract admiration and love, the tattooee being able to exert a positive influence over others.

Integral to the importance of tattooing is the skill and know-ledge of the tattooist. These days the art has become diluted with various practitioners taking up the needle, yet there are still highly respected master tattooists who preserve the tradition in all its seriousness and arcane lore. Some may claim to be mediums and make tattoos while possessed by the spirit of a *reushi* (ascetic). In this case they wear a mask in the traditional likeness of a hermit. In spite of such variations there are common essential elements.

Typically, as with other traditional arts and skills, a serious and respected tattooist will have gone through a lengthy apprenticeship in a master-pupil relationship. One present-day practitioner talks of studying for 10 years. 'First, I had to study the characters of the *khom* (ancient Khmer) alphabet, then learn *katha* (magic spells) and various types of *na* and *yan* (occult writing) until I knew them all by heart. To steady my hands, my teacher made me practise dry-tattooing on banana trunks for a long time.'

Steady hands are indeed needed as modern electric needles are not favoured by Thai tattooists. Instead a simple pointed steel or brass rod is used. Holding the needle in one hand and using the other as a rest for the point, the tattooist rhythmically jabs at the skin, pricking out the pattern with no other guidance. Pride in one's work is not the only the reason for a sure hand; a mistake in the tattoo is consid-ered very unlucky.

Nowadays the ink, usually dark blue, very occasionally red, is of a commercial type. In the past, however, tattooists would make their own ink according to recipes akin to a witch's brew – the fat from the chin of a corpse was one ingredient considered especially potent, best taken from seven bodies on a full-moon night.

Tattoo designs are most commonly animals (double-tailed lizards are popular), figures from classical Thai mythology and magic spells written in ancient Khmer script. The precise details of the designs, and especially the written spells and magic symbols which can be quite complex, are largely individually acquired by the tattooist and have greater or lesser effect depending on his knowledge.

Each session of tattooing usually takes no more than 10–15 minutes, though it is a lengthy process in that the tattooee will return time and again for a design to be completed, or to have others added.

It would also appear that there is safety in numbers. Those who favour tattoos these days tend to keep adding to their collection until most of the upper body is covered. In theory, however, there is no extra power implied in the number of tattoos and it is believed, for example, that a single dot placed correctly on the face by a master can give protection to the entire head.

The form of a tattooing session illustrates the respect and quasi-religious nature of the practice. The tattooee will bring the tattooist a small offering, as is done with monks, as well as the tattoo fee, usually no more than 100 baht or so. He will make the traditional *wai* greeting while kneeling reverently in front of the master, a position maintained throughout the tattooing.

The most important stage of the session is at the end. Tattoos in themselves have no power, no effectiveness in giving protection, they must be activated, as it were, by the tattooist – hence the awe in which the best masters are held. The power is conferred by the tattooist mumbling some incantation, then blowing on the tattoo. A sword may also be ritualistically used to smite the tattoo in confirmation of its effectiveness – not, incidentally, done with such force as to actually prove invulnerability.

The tattooist will also proffer moral advice. This again exemplifies the spiritual nature of tattooing and the emphasis not on the tattoo per se but on the relationship between tattooist and tattooee. That is why the meanings of designs, spells and diagrams are mostly irrelevant (in fact they are obscured by time). The significance lies in the process and practice, not the object.

As in most supernatural belief, the magical power implied in an object is reciprocated by an obligation on behalf of the subject. Should the tattooee fail to follow the advice of the tattooist, or commit some sin, or generally behave badly, the power of the tattoo will be diminished or completely destroyed. Moreover, the power should be replenished by attending the tattooist's annual *wai kru*, a widespread Thai ceremony held to honour a master or teacher – essentially the relationship between tattooist and tattooee is that of master and student.

As one tattooist comments, 'They (tattooees) are not to verbally abuse other people's parents, nor to make obscene gestures towards others. In addition, they are instructed to replenish this power by regularly chanting specific spells taught to them by the masters.'

Conveniently such reciprocal demands can be used to explain away a tattoo that fails to offer protection. Should the bullet or knife, say, strike home, then the tattooee must have done something bad and thus destroyed the protective power of his body markings.

On the other hand, it is the occasional story of an amazing escape which 'proves' the effectiveness of spiritual tattoos. Should someone miraculously survive a dangerous situation or an accident relatively unharmed, people will say it was because of magical power.

It is easy for the modern mind to scoff at such ideas, yet there is a certain logic behind the working of a tattoo. If the tattooee senses danger he is supposed to still his mind and recite the magic spell appropriate to his tattoo. This is said to awaken the guardian spirit, but more rationally it aids clear-headedness and thus, with greater awareness, the person may be better able to avoid impending harm.

To the outsider confronted with the supernatural, there is always the question 'does it work?' When you see half a dozen young men freely giving up a Sunday afternoon to receive a magical tattoo, or the crowds who flock to the annual *wai kru* at Wat Bang Phra in Nakhon Pathom, the question becomes immaterial. If western tattoos are a matter of beauty being in the eye of the beholder, traditional Thai tattoos are a case of power in the mind.

A CHARMED LIFE

Following a number of unexplained deaths among their colleagues, Thai workers overseas were, at the suggestion of Thailand's deputy interior minister, to be sent amulets and charms donated by the public.

'In times when we still do not know the real cause of the problem, we should boost their morale by giving them amulets and charms,' the deputy minister was reported as saying.

The anecdote is not ancient history, rather it was reported in the *Bangkok Post* of March 24, 1990. Curious though the idea may be, the custom of wearing or keeping protective charms remains widespread in Thailand. See virtually any Thai male in an open-neck shirt and you'll likely glimpse a gold-encased amulet, even a cluster of them, strung on a necklace.

A belief in the protective power of amulets and charms is an ancient one but it has lost little of its potency or popularity in the modern age. The idea predates Buddhism and while many amulets have come to be associated with the national religion, in the nature of the image itself and in the object's blessing by a monk, it is not strictly a Buddhist concept.

Ancient societies the world over, faced with often baffling natural and mysterious forces, commonly put faith in various objects which were believed to impart some degree of protection against potential harm from the unknown and the capricious. Such practices do not vanish in the wake of cultural advancement and organized religion. They may be overlaid by civilization but not necessarily obviated by it.

As E.O. James wrote in a 1961 study of comparative religion, 'The thought and practice of civilized peoples cannot be cut off as with a knife from the underlying customs and beliefs which have played a determining part in shaping the resulting products, however much subsequent knowledge and ethical evaluation may have modified and transformed the earlier customs.'

Rabbit's foot talismans, St Christopher medallions as protection for travellers and such like are illustrations of the persistence of supernatural beliefs in the West. In Thailand both Buddhist and secular charms and amulets are manifestations of a similar phenomenon.

Referred to collectively as *khawng-khlang*, 'sacred potent objects', Thai amulets are found in many forms. Undoubtedly the most popular are those with images of the Buddha. Known as *phra khruang-rang*, these come in many shapes and sizes, depicting the Buddha in all four of the classic postures, though typically in the seated position. With close to a thousand different kinds, they represent a miniature gallery of Buddhist sculpture.

Buddha amulets are classified into various categories depending not only on the image itself but also on the materials used, the shape and the date of issue. In size they can vary between two and seven centimetres (one and three inches) high. They may be cast from metal or carved out of wood, ivory or resin, though most often they are made of fine clay, pressed in a mould and fired in a kiln.

Although clay is the usual material, it is a more complex medium than first appears, being mixed with all sorts of strange ingredients – different kinds of flower pollen, incense, chewed areca nut, ashes of burnt sacred texts and other unexpected substances. The amulet's power is in part derived from its association with powerful things, hence the importance of the ingredients that go into its making. The manufacture of Buddha amulets is largely done by senior monks, although laymen are not excluded. However, it is a tricky matter as considerable knowledge of the proper ingredients, as well as of magic spells and sacred scripts is required.

Almost as popular as the Buddha amulets are those which depict the head of a famous monk or other highly revered personage, the most popular and respected among the latter being King Chulalongkorn, Rama V. Made in the form of metal medallions, these differ from the clay charms in being manufactured commercially, often at the commission of some fund-raising committee.

Besides Buddha amulets and medallions there is a host of other charms which reputedly protect the wearer against all manner of harm. 'It would be possible to write a biggish book about charms to ward off sword or bullet wounds. There are dozens of different kinds – tattoo marks, written formulas, knotted strings, tiny images of Buddha, precious stones, dried seeds, needles in the body, and others too numerous to mention,' W.A.R. Wood noted in his charming 1965 book of reminiscences, *Consul in Paradise*.

Way back in the past, the earliest forms of amulets were strange objects found in nature. These included pebbles, cat's eye stones, solid pig's teeth, pliable iron, certain kinds of plants and such like that were deemed to have supernatural powers simply because they were rare – hence miraculous – occurrences in nature.

Evolving with time was the belief in the protective power of objects of non-natural, manufactured origin. Two of the most widespread of these in Thailand are *takrut* and *phlad khik*. The latter is a phallic symbol, generally carved from wood and worn either around the neck or hung from a belt. Traditionally these were given to small boys as protection against snake bites and to ward off evil spirits. They were also favoured by merchants who believed they had the power to boost business. Today, they are popular among men of all ages and are almost as common as Buddha amulets.

The amulet known as *takrut* is a thin sheet of metal, perhaps gold though more often copper, tin or lead, on which are inscribed sacred or magical inscriptions. It is then rolled like a cigarette into a small cylinder, strung on a gold or silver chain, or a cotton string and worn, like the *phlad khik*, as protection against various ills. Minute versions of the charm were also inserted beneath the skin, where they were supposed to move around the body, protecting any spot from being pierced by a bullet or knife.

All amulets, both Buddha images and secular objects, are designed to give the wearer protection in one form or another. Apart from bringing general good luck, they may have specific functions, such as the ability to survive accidents or acts of violence. In addition they are supposed to impart a sense of well-being, giving confidence and the desire to behave well. Thus the charm is indirectly effective in promoting a person's overall prosperity and popularity.

Buddha amulets are considered more sacred if they have been made by an especially revered monk. Nonetheless, with the exception of those oddities found in nature, and thus automatically powerful, all amulets need to be blessed before they are fully effective.

Blessing can take various forms. At its simplest it is accomplished when a monk gives a Buddha image to a layman. Taking the object in both hands, the monk murmurs a short magical formula or spell in *pali*, and afterwards blows sharply on the amulet. Having received the amulet, the layman should then briefly press it against his forehead as a mark of appreciation.

A much more elaborate ceremony, at which anyone can have amulets blessed, may be officially organized and presided over by a number of monks. Such rituals are held in temples on especially auspicious days and take as their essential element the concentrated power of the monks in attendance.

While the wearing of amulets is not preached in Buddhist teachings, the practice does relate to the religion's emphasis on correct conduct. Regardless of how potent an amulet may be claimed to be, and no matter how well it has been blessed, its power will be weakened or destroyed if its wearer behaves badly. This also provides a handy escape clause if an amulet fails to protect – it was the fault of the owner not the object.

Amulets are supposedly more potent if they are given rather than bought. Then, however acquired, they should be cared for properly. When putting on a necklace of amulets, for example, it is proper to raise it to the forehead while uttering some invocation, such as asking for the 'Protection of the Buddha, of the Law and of the Monkhood'. Never should amulets be put in a low position where they may be stepped on, as this would be an insult. When washing or using the toilet, the wearer should place the charms behind his back or in his mouth so as not to give offence.

Among other ways in which offence may be given is letting the amulet come into contact with female nether garments. A women wearing amulets should remove her sarong by lowering it, not pulling it over the head. By the same token, anyone wearing charms should not walk beneath women's garments that may be hung up. An amusing anecdote illustrates unfortunate repercussions from failing to observe this point.

A folk tale from Phetchaburi relates how a boy's mother had washed her sarong and hung it out to dry before going off to work in the fields. It then began to rain and the little boy, wearing an amulet around his neck, saw the sarong and went to unhook it from the line with a pole. To do so he had obviously to step under the garment; as he did so the pole jerked up of its own accord and whacked the lad on the forehead in rebuke.

The moral of the story is that the protective power of amulets, like that of virtually all superstitious beliefs, is reciprocal – the object must be treated with respect if its power is to be beneficial.

So, what do amulets offer when properly cared for? Dr Voravit Clovutivat, a distinguished plastic surgeon who is also a well-known collector of amulets and an authority on the subject, has spoken of two incidents experienced by friends. In one a colleague won six lottery prizes shortly after a monk had given him an amulet.

Rather more remarkable is the story of another friend who survived a serious car crash with only minor injuries. He habitually wore several amulets and noticed after the accident that these had disappeared, yet their containing frames still hung from the gold chain around his neck. It was his belief that the amulets had gone out to protect him.

Dr Voravit himself is noncommittal on the subject. 'These things cannot be proven. Nor are they guaranteed,' he said in a public lecture. 'People decide for themselves, mainly through their own experiences or those of people they trust. Also, some amulets may demonstrate their power for some, yet not for others no matter how long they may have them.'

As a keen collector, Dr Voravit is more concerned about protecting his amulets than having them protect him. This is scarcely surprising since amulet trading has become a multi-million baht business. Trade is brisk at Bangkok's main amulet market at Wat Mahathat, and similar trading places are found in almost every province. The popularity of collecting is such as to sustain at least half a dozen specialist magazines devoted to the subject. There are even amulet-showing competitions.

Age, rarity, popularity and beauty are all factors that affect an amulet's price but the major criteria are the fame and reputed power of the monk who made it. With the best pieces changing hands for a million baht or more, it is not surprising that fakes abound. As with gemstones, collectors need experience and knowledge – perhaps also magical protection – to avoid pitfalls.

THE SPIRIT REALM

In late 1992, the Thai staff at the British Embassy in Bangkok became concerned about what can only be described as the height of diplomacy. They feared that the then ambassador, Christian Adams, was too tall.

At 1.93 metres (six foot four inches), His Excellency towered over the embassy's spirit house and this was considered a bad omen, upsetting the compound's guardian spirits who in disgust, it was claimed, had knocked their low-lying abode sideways and cast a spell of sickness over the entire mission. So, in a novel showing of esprit de corps, the embassy built a new spirit house raised just above the ambassador's height, and all was well again.

What makes this more than a curious anecdote of the diplomatic life is the vivid way it illustrates the importance Thais attach to the spirit world. A belief in spirits and ghosts has been common to virtually all peoples throughout the world at all times and the Thais are no exception. In a paper written for the Siam Society some years ago, scholar A.J. Irwin commented: 'There is no doubt that among most classes of people in this country [Thailand] beliefs are held in the existence of spirits good and bad, both of this world, and, to a much more limited extent, of other worlds.'

The most obvious manifestation of such beliefs is the ubiquitous spirit house. Like the one at the British embassy, these are found in the compounds of virtually every home, office, hotel and public building, even in front of today's high-tech high-rises. Typically in the form of model temples or traditional Thai wooden houses, they may be large or small, simple or ornate, but none are merely decorative and all serve a precise and practical function.

According to popular Thai belief, a guardian spirit, known as *Phra Phum* (Lord of the Land) occupies the site of any building and watches over the fortunes of those who live or work there. In order to ensure its continued protection, the spirit should be properly housed and shown due respect. If not, any manner of ill luck may befall the human residents of the land.

The choice of style of spirit house is an individual preference but only an expert in such matters, generally a Brahman priest, can properly answer the question of its location. The site should face either south or north, both auspicious directions, and it should not be overshadowed by the building lest the spirit refuse to take up residence. A post is then erected on the chosen spot and the little house is placed on top accompanied by an elaborate ceremony in which food, fruit, flowers, candles and incense are laid before the shrine in invitation for the spirit to make its home there and protect the property and its new residents.

The spirit house itself comprises a single room and small outer terrace at a slightly lower level where daily offerings can be put. Placed inside the shrine is a picture or image symbolic of *Phra Phum*, usually depicted with a doubled-edged sword in its right hand and sometimes a book in the left (used, it is believed, to record the deaths of people under the spirit's protection). Figures of people and animals may also be placed in the shrine to serve *Phra Phum*.

As with other supernatural beliefs, spirit houses imply a reciprocal relationship with the unknown and the invisible. In return for its acquiescence and assistance, the spirit must be fêted with daily offerings of food and flowers, served always in the morning along with burning incense. Special offerings should also be made on important days such as the anniversary of the shrine's installation and New Year's Day.

In order that the shrine's protection be constant, due respect must be accorded and *Phra Phum* treated as one would a host. When a guest arrives, for example, he or she should first ask for permission to stay the night and for protection before going to sleep. The latter is in the belief that otherwise sleep would be disturbed by nightmares and evil spirits would come to sit on the guest's chest, causing difficulty in breathing. Likewise, on departure the guest will say farewell to the spirit house and request a safe journey.

The reciprocal nature of the relationship between owner and spirit house is ongoing. If the human residents enjoy good fortune, for instance, being able to afford a new car or a higher standard of living, the spirit house should similarly be improved or enlarged. Conversely, if there is a premonition of misfortune, or a desire to overcome some difficulty, the spirit may be asked to help and be rewarded with a special offering should the prayer be granted.

The realm of the supernatural is, of course, not limited to individual properties and the influence of spirits extends over whole villages and cities. Notably, every Thai town will have a *lak muang*, or 'city pillar', which both marks the town's founding and serves as the residence of its guardian spirit. Shrines may also be erected to individual spirits, such as that of *Chao Mae Tuptim*, located on the site of Bangkok's Swissotel Nai Lert Park and famous for its preference for offerings of model phalluses.

Such spirits may be held in considerable awe. 'Because of its important status,' comments anthropologist B.J. Terwiel, 'many devotees treat the guardian spirit of the town pillar with respect which in some cases borders on trepidation.'

The significance attached to city pillar spirits was vividly illustrated by a report in the *Bangkok Post* of November 23, 1991, describing a visit by Thailand's then Army Commander-in-Chief to the City Shrine in the southern town of Nakhon Si Thammarat. Quoting 'well-informed sources', the newspaper article related that during the ceremony, the spirit of the guardian of the City Shrine had advised the army chief through a medium not to resist the popular demand for a democratic constitution 'otherwise he might encounter a fateful event'.

The origins of the spirit house in Thailand are obscure, some experts holding that the custom was prevalent amongst T'ai peoples as early as the 10th century, before they began migrating from southern China. The Thais themselves explain the reason behind spirit houses in a rational and endearing fashion. When asked why, they will smilingly reply, 'We are taught to be good to our neighbours, so why can't we be generous to the spirit who is living in our own home.'

The unseen but accommodated and respected guardians of homes, villages and cities are but the most obvious inhabitants of Thailand's vastly populated spirit world. Irwin notes that 'the subject of spirits – the belief in them, and the worship of them – is a very wide one,' and countless spirits are referred to in Thai by the general term *phi*. Added to the generic name are other titles which denote specific spirits. There is, for example, *phi krasu*, which is similar to the ugly hag of the archetypal European witch.

Generally, as described by Irwin, there are three broad categories of *phi*, each with its own innumerable specific types. Guardian spirits are classed as *phi ruen*, while another category, *phi lawk*, include what are usually meant by the word 'ghost' in English. *Phi lawk* are spirits of dead persons who haunt a locality or appear in certain houses. According to Irwin, they 'always appear with the intention of misleading and frightening people, and seem to have the power of making their presence not only seen but felt. For instance, a *phi lawk* might sit on the end of your bed, and pull your toes.'

Both *phi ruen* and *phi lawk* are deemed to inhabit the earth, but a third, less common, category of spirits is spoken of as dwelling in heaven or hell. Chief among such *phi*, says Irwin, is *Tau-wet-suwann*, the master of all spirits and described as a *yaksha* (mythical giant) living in heaven. One of the supposed attributes of a *Tau-wet-suwann* is the power to cast a certain charm which inflicts smallpox on children.

Less publicly acknowledged than celestial spirits and guardian spirits, though no less prevalent, are malevolent *phi* which can be troublesome, entering a person's body and taking possession. The existence of such annoying spirits has given rise to a whole variety of shamans and exorcists, sometimes Buddhist monks but more often lay people, who are recognized as possessing the power to control, or at least influence, the spirit world.

Irwin gives a detailed account of a not untypical case of spirit possession and its exorcism:

'A certain official in a government department, about two hours after eating his evening meal, arose and began talking wildly and nonsensically, threatening to pull the house down, and generally behaving like a lunatic. His friends tried to calm him, but at last seeing plainly that an evil *phi* had entered into him, they proceeded to call in a witch doctor to drive away the demon. The doctor took an ordinary iron nail, and pressed the point of it very lightly down on the upper part of the last joint of one of the patient's big toes. The afflicted man, who was being held by his friends, instantly howled as if in pain, as though his toe was being pierced through. In reality the point of the nail hardly made an impression on the skin. The doctor then seized the toe, and squeezed it hard with the intention of forcing the *phi* through the hole supposed to have been made by the nail. He then took the nail, and drove it into a piece of wood in entering which it was supposed to pass through the body of the demon, and thus cause it to be destroyed, or to enter into the nail. The latter was then hurled far away. Within fifteen minutes of this ceremony the patient completely recovered his senses and normal condition.'

Although Irwin was writing of some years ago, similar cases of possession and subsequent exorcism, albeit varied in detail, are still common today. The 'witch doctor' mentioned by Irwin should not be understood in the pejorative English sense; such practitioners – shamans, exorcists, call them what you will – command respect among Thais for their powers and the service they provide.

The act of exorcism differs from shaman to shaman. Some are extremely theatrical, while others are less dramatic and generally employ the simple elements of fire and water, which are an anathema to spirits. Fire is commonly in the form of a bunch of lighted candles which the shaman waves around the subject. Water, sometimes perfumed with jasmine, is poured over the patient, either in a token sprinkling or a complete dousing.

Often the spirit talks through the voice of the possessed and a dialogue may be held with the shaman, the latter, for example, promising the spirit peace and rest if only it leaves the body it has taken over. Such exchanges may be amusing, although people do become frightened if a spirit threatens violence.

Serious cases of possession are commonly dealt with in private consultations between the shaman and the afflicted person, usually accompanied by one or two relatives or close friends. Other forms of exorcism are communal events, which may perhaps be more accurately described as spiritual re-charge sessions. That is to say, the subjects are not obviously possessed by a malevolent *phi* but nonetheless feel rundown, in need of a psychic boost.

Such exorcisms are mass affairs and I have seen more than one hundred people, men and women, young and old, turn out on a Sunday afternoon to take part. The shaman or exorcist in these cases is quite often a Buddhist monk, especially revered for possessing psychic powers. Typically the participants line up and proceed to sit one by one in front of the monk who splashes water over them, mumbles some incantations and firmly prods various parts of their body with a baton. If an individual appears somewhat distressed, lighted candles may also be used in the ritual. Each exorcism or spiritual re-charge takes but a minute or two, and afterwards the 'patients' do look refreshed, relieved, more relaxed or in some other way appear to have benefited from the experience.

Allied to exorcists and fulfilling an equally valued role are mediums, people who are capable of going into a trance and allowing themselves to become possessed by a benevolent spirit. Under this influence they perform acts of healing and similar services aimed at promoting the physical and mental well-being of their clients.

Mediums, commonly but not exclusively women, may take up the profession by choice, through study and meditation, but with many others the decision is pressed upon them, often after a protracted illness which may be diagnosed as caused by a reluctance to serve a spirit.

Spirit possession is the essential attribute of all mediums, although there is enormous variation in the style and manner in which it is expressed. Some mediums are seemingly ordinary housewives who quietly enter a trance in their own unadorned living room. Others cultivate an element of showmanship and prefer a more dramatic approach, dressing outlandishly and employing 'magic' swords and other props in an exotic quasi-religious setting.

The more flamboyant mediums typically put on spectacular displays during special ceremonies at which devotees gather to pay homage. Not long ago, one of the most renowned mediums in Bangkok, a young man named Wanchai who claimed possession by a powerful spirit enamoured of the Hindu gods Siva and Kali, achieved such superstar status that he held a twice-yearly parade through the streets around his home. Highlighting these processions were acts of self mortification during which the medium pierced his cheeks and tongue with skewers and performed other similar feats to demonstrate his supernatural powers. Thousands of devotees followed the parade, some seeking to touch the 'master' as a measure of good luck.

Less gruesome but equally colourful and flamboyant are the spirit dances held in the northern province of Chiang Mai. These are annual mass meetings of mediums who gather to dance in honour of their tutelary spirits. The mediums, men and women dressed in vividly coloured traditional costume, first pay respects to their spirit masters, then begin to dance individually, sometimes swaying to the typical Thai folk rhythm of the *ramwong*, or gyrating to pop sounds as the band switches tempo between the customary and the contemporary. Possession does not normally accompany the dance and is usually entered into afterwards, when clients may consult the mediums.

Regardless of the ritual and the differing styles of practice, all mediums are recognized as receiving special powers from spirit possession and are central figures in the various spirit cults which continue to thrive in Thailand. Indeed, there is evidence that there are more mediums today than in the past, and what was once a rural phenomenon is finding increasing popularity among city dwellers. Much of this has to do with the reasons why people consult mediums.

Essentially and traditionally mediums combine the roles of doctor and psychiatrist or community counsellor and are consulted about both physical ailments and mundane problems, such as affairs of the heart. Today, the stresses and strains of modern society have opened up fresh scope for the medium.

After studying spirit cults in northern Thailand, academic Walter Irvine has concluded: 'The mediums frequently define themselves as healers, but it is my strong impression that curing accounts for less than half of the consultations. These are mostly related to the recently internalized values of individual material achievement and to status and economic needs. For instance, when dissatisfied with a job or when unemployed, a person can seek the power of a medium's possessing spirit to become successful. Also, a medium's power can be used to influence the social superior favourably and ensure his patronage [a vital element in Thai social dynamics], or it can discover the winning number in a lottery draw.'

From the evidence of various studies, it would seem that the pressures of modern society are revitalizing interest in mediums and spirit cults. Nonetheless, age-old occult practices still have a part to play and some mediums specialize in very traditional services. There is a form of black magic, for instance, in which it is believed a victim may be attacked by an enemy and become invisibly inflicted by a foreign object, perhaps a nail or tuft of hair, magically implanted in his or her body. When this happens the subject will feel pain which can only be cured by a medium possessing the power to remove the object and break the spell.

A Bangkok-based specialist in this field performs in a way akin to a conjuring act. As he chants magic spells he passes an ordinary hen's egg over the victim's body in order to detect the spot where the foreign object has lodged itself. When the egg touches the area it will leap out of the medium's hands. He takes another ordinary egg and holds it over the affected area and magically draws out the cause of harm. To prove it he cracks open the egg and there amid the yolk is an old rusty nail or whatever.

A conjuring trick? Perhaps, but scores of people visit this medium every day and their expressions of relief after treatment indicate they believe otherwise.

SMARTER THAN
I THOUGHT

I am smart, clever and have a brain full of information. I'm serious. What I mean is I am a serious kind of person. I know all this not because I am clever but because I was told so by Mr Duang Suriya Ntheat, president of the Thai Federation of Astrologers. This elderly avuncular gentleman read all about me from my face within a minute or so of our first meeting. Not all was flattering, but that's another story. The point is, fortune-telling is big in Thailand.

Devoutly Buddhist though the country is, a belief in the supernatural sits comfortably with the national religion. The ancient Brahman divinatory system persists and court astrologers still calculate the auspicious dates and times for royal rituals.

On the mundane level, some 60 per cent of the population, according to the Thai Astrologers' Association, habitually consults fortune-tellers. People commonly set the dates of weddings, business deals and other major undertakings according to favourable astrological aspects. They also seek advice on all manner of doubts and questions – from success in scholastic exams to marriage prospects and investment potential – as they look for assurance and ways to anticipate the future.

Meeting the demand in Bangkok are an estimated 10,000 professional fortune-tellers, practising variously astrology, face-reading, palmistry and card-reading using either ordinary playing cards or tarot decks. Among other more arcane systems are reading the soles of the feet and finding winning lottery numbers in tree blossoms.

'Each method has its own, different kind of accuracy,' Mr Duang claims. 'Palm reading is good if you want to know about work and success. The face tells you about character, while cards are effective for knowing what's going to happen in the future.'

Having consulted three fortune-tellers, each employing a different guiding system, I have to admit to a certain consistency. My horoscope, drawn up by Banglampoo-based astrologer Mrs La-eard Pongpruksa, indicated the same problems of stress and tiredness that Mr Duang had warned me about. Mrs La-eard did also say I would be helped by some older person with 'a yellow skin and wide forehead' some time round about now.

In a remarkably astute horoscope and tarot reading, Mrs Phatcharavan Kasemsant Na Ayutthaya at 'Isis' on Soi Thonglor summed up my current psychological state and immediate prospects with unnerving accuracy for someone who had never met me before. 'It's really all about your potential,' she explained. 'I don't advise people to have their fortune told. I don't know any more than my clients do, but I can act as a kind of mirror.'

Rather than telling you whether you're going to meet a tall, dark stranger, or pick the winning lottery number, Thai fortune-telling seems more a question of personal advice, providing a 'mirror', in Mrs Phatcharavan's description. In this way you may come to see your personal situation more clearly and so make wiser decisions about the course of your life.

As another astrologer put it, 'Fortune-tellers are like psychiatrists. They make suggestions as to where to redirect one's life if it's going astray. For example, if parents can't decide what they'd like their child to study, and the student can't either, they may all go to consult a fortune-teller. We are the supporting, behind-the-scenes factor in a person's life.'

There is an implied belief in fate but if the future cannot be changed, it may be modified to a degree or turned to greater advantage through the advice of a fortune-teller. 'We may not be able to erase fate,' an astrologer told me, 'but we can help reduce the impact of the misfortune. For instance, if a person is fated to meet with an accident, I might tell him or her to avoid driving or travelling a long distance. The outcome could possibly be a milder accident at home.'

The concept of a fortune-teller as a kind of psychologist or spiritual doctor is deeply embedded in Thai culture and among rural communities mental well-being has traditionally been treated by the village *mor doo*, 'divinatory doctor', literally one who 'sees'. Today, the growing sophistication of modern city society has not, as might be expected, made the *mor doo* redundant. On the contrary, practitioners themselves have simply become more sophisticated and better educated. It is quite possible, for example, to have your palm read by someone holding a MBA.

The same applies to the people who visit fortune-tellers. They are not necessarily the nervous or the simple-minded; they come from all classes, from taxi drivers to university graduates and politicians. In the case of well-known figures, local newspapers often report on their astrological concerns, as with the case of a top army officer who made no secret of consulting an astrologer over the appropriate time for him to leave the military and enter politics.

Fortune-telling not only survives in the modern Thai world, it thrives. Mr Duang said more people are consulting fortune-tellers now than ever before as a result of the greater stresses and strains of today's fast-paced life, and the increased uncertainty people face in changing times.

Nobody looks askance at the fortune-telling habit; it is simply another example of the Thai approach to life and its problems. 'While Western people rush to psychiatrists' offices when they have problems, Thais consider those who do so hopelessly insane, believing a fortune-teller to be more reliable than a therapist,' said Woraphan Laohawilai, president of the Thai Astrologers' Association.

As a further point to ponder, she noted that psychiatrists have it easy because patients tell them everything, while astrologers are not told anything but are expected to offer revelations.

The popularity of fortune-tellers is readily seen in the amazing variety of places you come across them. Throughout Bangkok you can find small shops advertising their trade with posters of a large palm or an astrology wheel, or just a woman with a pack of cards sitting on the sidewalk or under a tree in Lumpini Park. More upscale practitioners are found in the lobby of deluxe hotels or the concourse of plush shopping plazas.

Mostly these are anonymous practitioners, though there are renowned astrologers whose skills are so highly regarded that they have their own consulting rooms and clients need to make an appointment. There are also those with recognized specializations, known to be particularly successful in, for example, advising on romance, land deals or tracing lost valuables.

As to costs, readings can be bought for anything from the 50 baht asked for by an astrologer sitting under the tree in the park to a thousand baht or more charged by the top seers operating out of executive-style consulting rooms.

Providing training grounds for tomorrow's seers are the Thai Astrologers' Association, founded in 1947, and Mr Duang's Federation of Astrologers, both of which operate fortune-telling schools. Here, for a few hundred baht, anyone can enrol in an eight-month course that covers all facets of the divinatory arts. Each year, between them, they turn out some 500 qualified astrologers. Some of these graduates will become professional fortune-tellers, although the business world is increasingly realizing the potential of divination. Salespeople, for example, are beginning to cotton on to the possibilities.

'The key to selling is to know what type of person the customer is,' said one local insurance salesman who practises face-reading. 'For example, as soon as you see a potential buyer with thick eyebrows and bulging eyes, you know he is the hasty type and so you must get to the point right away. On the other hand, if the client has thin eyebrows and small eyes, you know he is very circumspect and you'll need several meetings before closing a deal.'

Clearly a modern slant on divination but then, although fortune-telling may be archaic as well as arcane, man's quest for assurance, if not insurance, has not altered appreciably over the centuries.

THE CEREMONIAL WORLD

From the simple charm of the wai *greeting to the sheer magnificence of a royal barge procession on the Chao Phraya River, from matters of social etiquette to the ways and means of expressing respect and devotion, there is endless fascination in the rich and varied facets of Thai ceremony and ritual.*

HELLO, GOODBYE

Nothing expresses so immediately and so charmingly the innate hospitality and grace of the Thais than the *wai*. Both a 'hello' and a 'goodbye', the *wai* is the universal Thai greeting that all visitors encounter throughout their stay in the country, from the cabin attendant's welcome as they board a THAI flight to their hotel receptionist's farewell when they depart.

Thais are delighted when a foreigner returns the gesture, even if the latter may not be aware of the full etiquette involved, which is more than readily appears as the *wai* is not exactly the equivalent of shaking hands. Besides a greeting and a farewell, the *wai* is a way of paying your respects, and the amount of respect you wish to convey, or think is due.

Simply, the *wai* is made by raising the hands, palms together, to a position lightly touching the body somewhere between chest and forehead. The head is slightly bent when *wai-ing* and the whole movement should be performed slowly and gracefully. There are, however, finer points to it. For example, the higher the hands are raised, the greater the respect shown. Thus when friends meet they'll position the hands around chest height because they are equals but if the person being greeted is of higher status or senior in age, the *wai* will be made with the finger tips around eye level and with a lower inclination of the head.

There is further etiquette involved in who initiates the gesture. Among social equals it is age, not sex, that counts and so a younger man will *wai* an older woman first. It is inappropriate for an older person to *wai* a younger person first, there being a superstition that such an action will take seven years off the latter's life. When it's a question of status, it is the junior who should initiate the *wai* before the senior returns the gesture. A Buddhist monk, incidentally, never returns a *wai* to a layman.

The most solemn and respectful *wais* are made to Buddha images, spirit houses and other sacred objects. It can be deeply moving to see devotees in a temple paying their respects to a Buddha image, kneeling and with the *wai* performed three times, the hands held high to the forehead, before bowing the head all the way to the floor. At other times performing the *wai* can be slightly disconcerting to see, as, for example, when your taxi driver takes both hands off the wheel to *wai* to the god Brahma as he passes the Erawan Shrine that stands at one of Bangkok's busiest traffic intersections.

The *wai* is not unique to Thailand; it originated India, where it is still practised, and was later adopted by Buddhist societies, the shape of the hands seen as representing a closed lotus bud, a Buddhist symbol of purity. However, the Thais, especially the women, are generally considered to perform the gesture more neatly and more gracefully than others, with a deep bow, sometimes a slight curtsy for women, and the arms drawn in close to the body.

The practised ease of the Thai *wai*, even when the circumstances are somewhat awkward, is well observed by Derek Tonkin in his 1990 book *Simple Etiquette in Thailand*. 'Watch,' he writes, 'a company Chairman responding to the *wai* made simultaneously by the members of his Board of Directors with his own collective *wai* while holding a bundle of papers in his right hand and his briefcase in his left hand, but somehow contriving to bring one hand close to the other without dropping anything.'

Although not an obligatory part of the custom, a smile certainly accentuates the charm of the *wai*. Thais smile a lot and it's become a travel brochure cliché to describe the country as the 'Land of Smiles'. Nonetheless, the smile is a reflex expression of the Thai's innate hospitality and the ingrained custom of welcoming strangers.

The social mores of the Thais are complex and, aside from welcoming, the smile stems in part from the convention that one does not cause another to lose face. That can at times be difficult to appreciate. For example, Thais will often smile when someone suffers a minor personal misfortune not because they are laughing at them but rather to show sympathy and a sharing of the misfortune.

The Thai smile can also be used to hide embarrassment, again with potential misunderstanding by the uninitiated, as when the driver of the car that has just bumped into yours gets out and smiles.

Of course, the Thais do smile at the comic and out of pleasure, and the smile is related to the concept of *sanuk*, literally 'fun' or 'joy', and the idea is that anything worth doing, work or play, should have an element of pleasure.

From greeting to masking uncertainty, nowhere more so than in Thailand does it help to smile.

If you're really someone – a VIP, honoured guest, or suchlike – you'll be greeted with not only a graceful *wai* and a beaming smile but also with a fragrant *malai*, the traditional Thai flower garland. These exquisitely strung rings of white jasmine flowers, usually given a dash of colour with rose petals, marigolds or orchids and finished with a tail of *dok rak*, literally 'love flowers', and local leaves, are said to symbolize the beauty of the Buddha's teachings and, because they are short-lived, the impermanence of life itself.

Yet the *malai* is not only a welcoming gift, it serves many functions and signifies many beliefs. From an offering to Buddha images or to spirit houses, to a token of respect to elders and distinguished guests, a floral decoration at weddings, or simply a natural air-freshener to hang on a taxi's rear-view mirror, the *malai*, in its beauty and delicacy, is a charming reminder of all things Thai.

THE ROYAL BARGE PROCESSION

In twenty years I've seen it on only three occasions. The Royal Barge Procession, held in the Thai capital on the Chao Phraya river, was long ago a regular feature of regal ceremonial but in the modern era this unparalleled pageant is staged only on rare historic occasions. November 4, 1999, was one of those times when the pages of history were turned back to reveal a sight of sheer royal splendour scarcely equalled in the world today.

For a few unforgettable hours on that afternoon the Chao Phraya, the 'River of Kings', was transformed into a glittering royal stage. In a blaze of colour and set against a backdrop of classical Oriental wonder, with the golden spires of the Grand Palace and venerable temples glinting in the sun, a procession of more than 50 ornate gilded royal barges, manned by over 2,000 traditionally costumed oarsmen, paraded down the river. Heading the procession was the swan-prowed *Suphanahong*, which conveyed His Majesty King Bhumibol Adulyadej, Rama IX, to Wat Arun for the Royal Krathin ceremony, the traditional presentation of monks' robes.

One of the climactic celebrations to mark His Majesty's 72nd birthday year and the auspicious completion of his sixth 12-year cycle, the pageant presented a picture of regal glory unchanged in essentials since the days of Ayutthaya.

'It is impossible to compare the beauty of the immense procession with two hundred boats,' wrote a European visitor to 17th-century Ayutthaya. 'The Royal barges travelled in twos in the front. All oarsmen have been trained to an admirable proficiency, dressed uniformly in gold-trimmed hats, tunic, knee and armbands. All rowing is in synchronized movement and rhythm. The oars, also of gold, touch the water with a sound that harmonizes with the boat song sung in praise of the King.'

The scale of the Royal Barge Procession is reduced today but otherwise this characteristically Thai pageant adheres strictly to tradition. The oarsmen still wear the costumes of medieval warriors, each stroke of the oars is dictated by a precise rhythm and accompanied by chanting, and the flotilla moves in stately unison according to a time-honoured formation. The vessels themselves, long sleek wooden craft, richly ornamented and distinguished by elaborate prows carved in the form of mythical creatures, are the same as in the past. The oldest of those seen today date from the reign of King Rama I (1782–1809), while others are faithful reconstructions of Ayutthaya-period barges, designed to preserve the glory of Thailand's golden age.

In addition to their historical significance, the Royal Barges are a quintessential part of Thai culture not only in their expression of the enduring role of the monarchy but also in their reflection of a characteristic way of life. The Thais have always lived along rivers and canals, houses were built facing waterways and life was largely dependent on waterborne transportation.

It has been that way since the 13th-century birth of the nation. Sukhothai had its canals, while Ayutthaya, on which Bangkok was originally modelled, had been an island city, located at the junction of the Chao Phraya, Lopburi and Pa Sak rivers. What served daily life was emphasized on festive occasions, and high water at the end of the rainy season was traditionally a time for river-borne celebrations and royal ceremonies. Still today the end of the annual rains is celebrated by boat races in many parts of the country.

Some historians trace the origin of the Royal Barges back to the first Thai capital at Sukhothai in the 13th and 14th centuries. But although there is some evidence that the early kings celebrated the Loy Krathong festival by boat, the Royal Procession as known today dates more surely from the Ayutthaya period (1350–1767). Royal Barges were then a prominent part of regal ceremonial, used not only for the Krathin ceremony but also during coronation celebrations and other state occasions, and as escorts greeting foreign missions arriving by ship on the Chao Phraya.

It was not entirely a matter of pageantry, however, and Royal Barges were originally warships used in river battles, as witnessed in the cannon ports which are still to be seen in the bows of today's vessels. The ceremonial use of barges in the past actually served a dual purpose: it was both a royal parade and a demonstration of the country's power. Peacetime processions thus served as occasions not only for pageantry but also for keeping the navy in constant readiness.

As Thailand entered the modern era and river battles became outmoded, the Royal Barge Procession remained a symbol of regal power. After the fall of Ayutthaya in 1767, when most of the barges vanished in the destruction of the city, the early kings of Bangkok ordered new vessels to be reconstructed as part of their aim to recapture the lost glory of the former capital. The barges were then regularly used in state ceremonies until the adoption of a constitutional monarchy in 1932. Tradition was struck a further blow during World War II, when the dry dock where the Royal Barges were stored suffered severe bomb damage.

Early in the present reign, His Majesty the King, always a keen preserver of cultural heritage, ordered a full renovation of the Royal Barges. Work was completed in time for a procession to be held on May 14, 1957, as part of the celebration of the 25th century of the Buddhist Era.

Subsequently, the barges have been periodically used for the Royal Krathin Ceremony and other nationally auspicious occasions, notably the Bangkok Bicentennial in 1982, His Majesty's 60th birthday in 1987 and the Royal Golden Jubilee in 1996. Each of these I have been lucky enough to see and each time they've held me spellbound. Nothing, not even any of Thailand's many other amazing rituals and festivals, can compare for sheer grandeur.

The barges vary in size from about 20 metres long to over 40 metres (65½ to 131 feet) and are manned by between 30 and 50 oarsmen. All are magnificent creations, each vessel being distinguished by its elaborate figurehead and with a canopied pavilion amidships, but the finest of all is the *Suphanahong*, reserved exclusively for conveying Their Majesties the King and Queen. With its figurehead fashioned in the shape of a swan (*hongsa*) and an intricately carved and gilded hull, this superb craft is 46.15 metres (151½ feet) long and 3.17 metres (10½ feet) wide, with a draft of 0.41 metres (16 inches) and a speed of 3.5 metres (11½ feet) per paddle stroke. Its crew consists of 50 oarsmen, two steersmen, two officers, seven canopy bearers, one flagman at the stern, one rhythm keeper and one boat songster who chants to the cadence of the oars.

Such has been the faithful preservation of the Royal Barges throughout history that on November 4, 1999 spectators were treated to a scene that would have been familiar to the Jesuit Father Tachard who, witnessing a reception in honour of a French mission in 1685, recorded: 'The long Royal Barge Procession that moved in an orderly fashion consisted of over 150 barges. Together with other boats, they covered the river as far as the eye could follow. It was a breathtaking sight. The sound of traditional chanting reverberated along both banks of the river which were crowded with people who were waiting to see the spectacular event.'

BRAHMANS

Easily recognized by their all-white dress and long hair tied back in a tight chignon, Brahman priests play an important role in Thai ceremonial and spiritual life. Their numbers are small, yet their influence far exceeds numerical strength and their services are called upon in the performance of all major royal ceremonies, as well as of numerous common rites and rituals ranging from the ancient custom of cutting the topknot to the blessing of a new house.

Brahmanism, the ancient religion of India and the forerunner of both Hinduism and Buddhism, is numerically the smallest of Thailand's minority faiths but in influence and meaning it is of the highest significance. In its strict form it is professed and practised by a few – lay and ordained alike – yet its gods, philosophy and rituals impinge directly on the system of Thai beliefs.

Today there are fewer than a dozen Brahman priests in Bangkok who are attached to the Royal Household and whose spiritual home – and physical abode in some cases – is the capital's one Brahman temple, the Deva Sathan, situated opposite the Giant Swing and adjacent to Wat Suthat.

The entire Brahman community of Bangkok comprises six families, or rather six surnames, and thus the numerical gauge is the extended rather than nuclear family. Even so their numbers are now a mere fraction of the countless Brahman priests who would have been found in Ayutthaya (the Ayutthaya era was Brahmanism's golden age in Thailand), and of the hundreds scattered around the country in the period prior to the introduction of a constitutional monarchy in 1932. A shrinking community, however, has not meant any lessening of the role of Brahmanism. Unofficial Brahman priests are widely found in upcountry communities where they are respected practitioners of many traditional rites rooted in Brahmanism.

Basically Brahmanism pays observance to a triumvirate of gods – Siva, Vishnu and Brahma – and to a whole pantheon of lesser deities. The religion originated in India and out of it grew, quite recognizably, Hinduism and, less obviously, Buddhism.

The term 'brahman' refers generally to the descendants of Indian migrants who came to South-East Asia more than 1,000 years ago. In the modern age, however, Brahmans in Thailand are effectively indigenous Thais despite a genealogical link with India. Certain characteristic physical features may be discerned but traces have diminished over the centuries since no female Brahmans accompanied the earliest migrants and intermarriage became a necessity.

Those who practise their religion today are known as Thai Brahmans and they have a duty, like Buddhist monks, to preserve the traditions of their faith.

Exactly when Brahmanism first came to Thailand and other parts of South-East Asia is uncertain in the absence of any surviving documentary evidence. It is believed, however, that contact was possibly first made as early as the second century BC, long before the Thais became dominant in the region. There were most likely two migratory routes; one overland via Myanmar and the other by ship across the Bay of Bengal and the Andaman Sea.

By the first or second century AD, the influence of Brahmanism – part of the process historians term the 'Indianization' of South-East Asia – was spreading widely throughout the region. It was eventually to take strongest hold in Cambodia where the Khmer of Angkor embraced it as it give substance to their belief in the semi-divine status of their kings. The impact of Indian culture also found royal favour in the kingdom of Srivijaya which held sway over what are now parts of Indonesia and southern Thailand between the 7th and 13th centuries.

When the Thais rose to power in the early 13th century and founded their first kingdom at Sukhothai, Brahmanism would have been well established in many parts of South-East Asia. Its most direct entry into mainstream Thai society would have been via the Khmer whose empire once included large areas of Thailand and whose cultural legacy was in part absorbed by the Thais as they emerged as a new sovereign power. The Khmer influence became even more pronounced in the 15th century when the second Thai kingdom, Ayutthaya, defeated Angkor and adopted many of its religious, political and cultural institutions.

In their rise to power the Thais had embraced Theravada Buddhism as their national religion. Yet there was never any conflict, and Buddhism and Brahmanism went hand-in-hand as the Thais shaped their spiritual life and the rituals and ceremonies that lent it substance.

The Thai monarchy most probably inherited the integral role of Brahmans in court life from the Khmer. It would probably have been retained initially partly to provide continuity in the beliefs of the population over which the new rulers extended their sovereignty. A further reason for the retention of Brahmanism was its function as a source of learning. Brahman priests had long been respected for their scholarship. During the process of 'Indianization' they had not only spread their beliefs but also given instruction in the *Phra Vedas* which cover all branches of knowledge, from the science of medicine and pharmacy to the laws that govern nations. Not least was the Brahmans' great learning regarding astrology.

While Brahmanism strengthened the concept of kingship through its concept of regal semi-divinity and afforded a valuable medium of learning, it did not clash with Buddhism. In fact, as the two religions have come to co-exist in the Thai system of beliefs, it is virtually impossible to separate the major tenets of Buddhism and Brahmanism.

The five precepts of Buddhism and its Four Divine States of Mind (*Phromvihara Si* – loving kindness, compassion, sympathetic joy and equanimity) are concepts equally held by Brahmanism and in part they originated from that earlier religion. Moreover, Buddhism has adopted much, in form as well as content, from Brahmanistic practices. Most obviously, the custom of holding candlelit processions around temples on major Buddhist festival days is a borrowing from Brahmanism, the belief being that anything within the circle of candlelight will be blessed. The Brahman usage of this is often seen at the pre-ordination ceremony of Buddhist monks when, in the home of the novice-to-be, a Brahman priest will ritualistically carry a lighted ceremonial candle around the celebrant and his family.

For their part, Brahmans hold that the Buddha was the ninth of 10 manifestations on earth of the god Vishnu. The Buddha is further respected for his attainment of Enlightenment.

Historically, the essential relationship between Brahmanism and Buddhism for the Thais has been a complementary one. Metaphysics and the concept of the world, heaven and hell are drawn largely from Buddhism, not from the theological and philosophical speculations of Brahmanism. In more practical matters, on the other hand, the ancient religious thought of India held considerable attractions.

As one commentator has written: 'The Thai elite draws heavily upon Hindu Brahmanical sources for authority and example in their search and attempt to sanctify and concretize the phenomenal order... Scriptures together with the Brahmans, the Hindu priests, whom Thailand inherited from the Khmers, provided the rites, the ceremonies, the festivals and the sacred cosmological myths, and they thus consecrate, embellish and complete Thai religious, cultural, social and political life.'

On the popular level, a deep reverence for Lord Buddha 'co-exists with a huge accretion of superstitious beliefs and practices. Daily life is, in fact, governed more by these beliefs than by the more sublime teachings of Buddhism. In this complex coterie of popular beliefs and superstitions an important position has been assigned to the Brahmanical elements.'

Chief among Brahmanical influences is its divinatory system (astrological notions and their impact on man's actions) and its host of *devas*, 'deities' or 'angels'. An obvious example of the role of the latter influence is the Erawan Shrine in Bangkok where the statue of Brahma is widely regarded as a potent source of good fortune, benevolently granting all nature of wishes.

But it is not only, or even essentially, the major gods of Brahmanism which impinge on the supernatural in Thai life. There is a catch-all inclusiveness with the *devas*, as anthropologist Robert Taylor illustrates: 'Often I have received a blessing from a doctor, monk or elderly layman, in which assistance or protection was supplicated on my behalf, first perhaps from the goodness of the Buddha, the Dharma [teaching or law] and the Sangha [monkhood]; then perhaps from certain Brahmanical deities mentioned by name; and finally from "all things sacred".' Taylor adds that the "all things sacred" is 'a sort of supernatural et cetera,' and 'clearly it is the Brahmanical sacred beings that are peculiarly subject to the et cetera notion.'

Existing in huge variety – both collectively, as with, for instance, *yakshas* (mythical giants) and *reushis* (holy hermits), and individually in figures such as Mother Water and so on – *devas* are supernatural beings characterized by a certain non-capricious predictability, dignity and augustness, and thus differ markedly from the legions of *phi*, or ghosts.

Basically, the *devas* are perceived as remote but benevolent deities who are protective rather than punitive and the attitude towards them is one of reverence. Belief in these deities is illustrated at most large festivals where an altar is set up, generally on the eastern (auspicious) side of the site, and arrayed with food, flowers and other offerings as an invitation for the *devas* to join the festival which will thus enjoy their protection.

A layman schooled in Brahmanical lore may perform such ritual, although royal and major festivals are presided over by Bangkok's small community of properly ordained priests, known as a *Dhavichat*, meaning twice born. The first birth is the natural one, the second comes with ordination, a ceremony that can only take place once a year at *Triyam Pavai*, the Brahman New Year, which, depending on the astrological charts, falls in either December or January.

The life of a Brahman ascetic is subject to few restrictions compared to that of a Buddhist monk. The hair must not be cut as it is a mark of acceptance of the ascetic life but otherwise a Brahman priest is free to follow a normal life – marry, have children and so on. While white is the official dress of Brahmans, other colours may be worn at ordinary times.

Daily routine is much the same as for the layman. A Brahman priest will usually awaken at 6 a.m. to pray. The daily recital of prayers is at the discretion of the individual but the amount of merit earned is proportional to the amount of devotional time. If no special rites are to be performed that day, the Brahman is at liberty to follow his own pursuits; priests belonging to the Royal Household have full-time employment as such, while others pursue ordinary occupations as their means of livelihood.

Traditionally the most important rites conducted by Brahmans relate to the monarchy and include coronation, royal weddings, oaths of allegiance and the annual ploughing ceremony. Priests also draw up astrological calculations to decide auspicious times for various ceremonies and undertakings. In former days they would also have interpreted a king's dreams and predicted the fortunes of battle.

Today there are seven major annual royal ceremonies at which Brahmans officiate: the Ploughing Ceremony (held at Bangkok's Phra Mane Ground in May and affording the visitor the best opportunity to see Brahmans in their official capacity); the anniversaries of His Majesty the King's birthday and coronation; the three ritual occasions on which the monarch changes the seasonal attire of the Emerald Buddha (the nation's palladium) and the celebration of the god Siva's annual visitation to earth (a festival that was formerly celebrated by spectacular – and dangerous – performances on the Giant

Swing which, though now unused, still stands in Bangkok).

Additional occasional royal ceremonies in which Brahmans are involved include the King's acceptance of a new white elephant, the birth of a royal child and a royal cremation (incidentally a rite of passage which Brahmans acknowledge by leaving their hair loose).

Within the Thai community at large, Brahmans are called upon to perform a variety of ceremonies, during which they recite incantations of invitation to the *devas* and make offerings of candles, incense and flowers. Spirits will also be appeased by lavish food offerings of most commonly a pig's head, as well as fish, chicken and other delicacies.

Common ceremonies at which such ritual is performed include the setting of a spirit house, the laying of a building's foundation stone, weddings, Buddhist monks' pre-ordination festivities and numerous other celebratory occasions at homes, offices, schools and shops when blessing is given through worship and propitiatory duties.

Once a widespread Brahman ritual though now in decline is the tonsure ceremony, the ritualistic cutting of a child's topknot. In the past, it was a popular custom for Thai infants to have their heads shaved, leaving just a tuft sprouting from the crown in anticipation of perhaps the single most important rite of passage in childhood, marked when the topknot was eventually cut, generally at puberty.

The ritual significance of haircutting is by no means limited to Thai culture. In his 1893 account of the tonsure ceremony, G.E. Gerini points out the religious importance of head shaving in ancient India and Egypt, and suggests it is impossible to decide in which civilization the practice originated, or whether, more likely, it evolved in both cultures independently. Moreover, he remarked on a widespread occurrence of the custom, citing examples of tonsure rituals not only in the Old World but also in Pre-Columbian Peru and Mexico.

In his early 20th century account of Thailand, W.A. Graham wrote, '... judging by the prevalence of a ceremony of tonsure in many widely separated parts of the world as an indication of a new phase of life or of the devotion of the individual to a set purpose, it is probably a manifestation of one of the most ancient customs of mankind.'

Essentially a Brahman rite, the tonsure ceremony signifies the passage from childhood to adolescence. In Hindu belief, it is through the skull beneath the tuft of hair that the human spirit enters the body at birth and departs at death. Accordingly, there is a belief that by covering this spot with a topknot a child has some kind of protection against accident or illness. Even now, when the practice is fast fading, parents may still decide a sickly child will benefit from having a topknot.

Traditionally the tonsure was ritualistically cut when a child approached puberty, usually between the ages of 11 and 13. These days it is more likely to be done earlier since children are afraid of being teased by their school friends for following such an old-fashioned practice. But whenever the topknot is removed, it must be at an odd-number age since even numbers are considered unlucky.

In the past, the most elaborate tonsure ceremonies were reserved for royalty – in the early 19th century, the rite for the future King Rama IV took seven days. Even in the case of commoners the occasion was marked by a three-day ritual.

First an auspicious date was set by a Brahman astrologer. This was a most important and tricky task as the chosen time had to be free of all possible evil or harmful influences and without any constellation bearing a female name visible in the heavens. As the day of the ceremony approached, the child's home was prepared by the setting up of an altar, the placing of Buddha images and the stringing of a sacred thread around the building to form a holy circle as protection against malevolent spirits. Around the altar shears, razors, bowls of holy water and other paraphernalia of the ceremony were put ready.

On the afternoon of the day but one before the actual hair cutting, friends visited the house bringing presents which were placed on the altar. Later monks arrived and after that the child duly appeared dressed in the finest clothes and jewels the family could afford. Accompanying were two or more Brahman priests who scattered rice and blew on conch shells.

The child then made obeisance before the monks, after which an end of the sacred cord protecting the house was attached to the topknot. A recital of Buddhist chants and prayers followed before the child retired. The day ended with a party of feasting and merry-making.

Recitations by the monks, and prayers and exercises performed by the Brahmans took up the second day. The third and final day began early and in silence so as to avoid attracting any evil spirits that might be about. The monks returned and the child appeared with the Brahman priests. When the propitious moment arrived the topknot was divided into three strands. The first was cut by the most honoured guest, the other two by the most elderly relatives present. A burst of drum-beating and music accompanied the operation, while after the three strands had been cut a barber finished the head-shaving in professional style.

Afterwards the child sat on a platform while the monks and guests poured lustral water over his head. The *Wien Thien*, or ritualized procession of lighted candles, was then performed. In the afternoon a purely Brahmanic ceremony was conducted to ensure the child's spirit did not take the occasion of the topknot cutting to desert the body.

For children whose parents still follow the custom, today's ceremony is a greatly abbreviated version of the traditional ritual. It may still take place in the home, though even the modern shortened version can be a costly affair and many families opt for a communal ceremony held annually at Bangkok's Brahman temple. But if no longer widespread, the tonsure ceremony is illustrative of one fundamental aspect of Thai supernatural belief that has a much wider relevance than just the topknot custom. This concerns the *khwan*, roughly translated as 'the essence of life' or 'spirit of life', the guardian spirit vital to all sentient beings. The *khwan* is supposed to reside in the physical body but it is a fragile presence and the spirit can leave at various moments, during sleep, illness or death, for example.

To contain the essence of life, to survive in an apparently alien world, has been a crucial concern of man ever since he began to explore his environment. In order to ensure the continued presence of this vital spirit, the Thais have a custom known as *tham khwan*, 'making' the essence of life. Not exclusively a Brahman ritual -- it may also be conducted by a respected relative or village elder, by a *mor khwan* ('soul doctor') or, occasionally, by a Buddhist monk – *tham khwan* is central to the tonsure ceremony. Other occasions on which it is conducted include times of illness or mental stress, the cutting of a baby's first hair, on the eve of ordination and during the wedding ceremony.

Diverse though they are, rites and rituals such as the *tham khwan* ceremony, the royal ploughing ceremony, or the commonplace laying of a foundation stone bear witness to the continued strength and on-going relevance of the ancient Brahmanical tradition which contributes yet a further complex weave to the fabric of Thai ceremonial and spiritual life.

A ROYAL CREMATION

On Tuesday April 9, 1985, Thailand paid its last respects to its much-loved late Queen Rambhai Bharni in a majestic cremation ceremony.

Tens of thousands of people ignored Bangkok's notorious summer heat and, as the mercury reached 38 degrees Celsius (100° Fahrenheit), flocked to the city's historic centre to witness the day-long rite presided over by the reigning monarch, King Bhumibol Adulyadej, Rama IX.

Queen Rambhai Bharni, wife of the late King Rama VII, was born in 1904 and spent 15 years in England, where the King had exiled himself after the bloodless revolution of 1932 transformed Thailand from an absolute to a constitutional monarchy. After her husband's death, the queen returned to Thailand in 1949 where she filled her days of retirement by supporting cultural activities and charity work.

On the day of the cremation, attention was focused on the Phra Mane Ground, adjacent to Bangkok's famous Grand Palace and Temple of the Emerald Buddha. At this time of the year, with the winds of the north-east monsoon prevailing, the area is a popular spot for the traditional pastime of kite-flying; none were soaring up into the sky that day.

The Phra Mane has been the royal cremation site for more than 200 years, ever since Bangkok was founded as the Thai capital in 1782, and for the first time in 30 years it was spectacularly trans-formed to serve its prime function.

The last royal cremation, that of the present King's grandmother, was held in 1956 and no more than 15 such rites were performed in that century. Thus, in addition to being a nation's final tribute, the event was a rare opportunity to watch one of Thailand's most important royal ceremonies, almost as significant as the coronation, in which Buddhist beliefs largely conquer the sting of death.

Queen Rambhai Bharni died on May 22, 1984. On her demise His Majesty King Bhumibol commanded that royal obsequies be observed as befitting her rank. For the following 11 months her body, encased in the *Phra Kosa Thong Yai*, a golden, bejewelled funeral urn first made for King Rama I, had been lying in state at the Dusit Throne Hall of the Grand Palace.

While religious rites were performed at specific intervals during the period, preparations for the actual cremation were begun the previous October under the supervision of the Fine Arts Department and other concerned organizations. Involved in the detailed work were 120 woodcarvers and other skilled craftsmen along with a further 150 carpenters and construction workers.

Public interest was soon stirred by an ornate, spired structure, resembling a miniature palace, gradually taking shape at the southern end of the Phra Mane Ground. This was the Golden Meru, the traditional crematorium of Thai royalty. Elsewhere, behind the scenes, craftsmen were busy fashioning statues of *devas* (angels), beautifully painted wood panels and a special urn made of fragrant sandalwood, while two old, exquisitely carved chariots of teak were undergoing expert restoration.

The Meru was revealed in its full splendour on April 9. Following the architectural style of what is known as a *prasat*, the Golden Meru royal funeral pyre has throughout recorded Thai history been constructed, with only minor variations, along a traditional design dictated by its inherent symbolism. To all appearances a small oriental palace, it is a cruciform building with entrances on the four sides, each sheltered by steep eaves.

On each side of the Golden Meru, stairways lead to the central chamber where the funeral urn is actually cremated. Around the base of the structure are statues of kneeling *devas* holding royal fans with a light inside.

With its archetypes dating back to the ancient Khmer civilization of Angkor, itself subject to Indian influences, the Golden Meru is a symbolic rendering of the cosmos. Meru is the name of the cosmic mountain where the gods dwell, mythically placed in the Himalayas. It forms the centre of the universe and is surrounded by seven concentric mountain ranges, separated from each other by seven seas. Indra, the king of the gods, inhabits a golden palace on top of the golden mountain, surrounded by the smaller palaces of the lesser gods. When a royal personage is cremated in the Meru, he or she is believed to be 'translated to the heavens'. In the Khmer Angkor civilization, mainly dominated by Hinduism imported from India, the Meru was a tacit statement on the divinity of kings.

Elements of Brahmanism (an ancient form of Hinduism) are incorporated in Buddhism, Thailand's national religion, particularly in royal rites such as cremations.

As well as being symbolic, the Golden Meru is also an ephemeral architectural form. It is built anew for each cremation, then dismantled after use, none of its parts ever being utilized for any other purpose.

Almost as traditional as the pyre itself is the carriage on which the funeral urn is conveyed to the cremation site. This is known as the Royal Great Victory Chariot, first used to bear the remains of King Rama I who died in 1809. Measuring 11 metres (36 feet) high and 18 metres (59 feet) long and weighing 40 tons, this impressive four-wheeled vehicle is made of carved wood, gilded and decorated with coloured mirror glass. It has a five-tiered base on top of which is a *busabok* throne to take the urn. The enormous carriage is drawn by around 300 soldiers, dressed in traditional costume, while, at the rear, a further 100 act as a brake.

The basic form of the cremation ceremony has been adhered to since the Ayutthaya period (1350–1767). However, for economy's sake, certain changes have been made in the 20th century. Most significantly these involve the size of the Meru and the concomitant expense of the ceremony. His Majesty King Bhumibol directed that rites for Queen Rambhai Bharni, while incorporating full honours, should be carried out at minimum cost. Even so, expenses for the entire ceremony have been estimated at around US$1 million.

The ceremonies begun early on April 9, with their Majesties the King and Queen presiding over religious rites at the Grand Palace. At 7.50 the first artillery gun salute boomed out and the firing continued to punctuate the morning.

The golden urn was placed on the chariot and, to the wail of conch shells and a funeral dirge on drums, trumpet and flute, performed by traditionally-dressed musicians, the procession was led by five battalions of troops, their full-dress uniforms making up blocks of vivid colour. The Royal Victory Chariot was preceded by a senior monk. HRH the Crown Prince followed, leading a procession of members of the royal family, Prime Minister Prem Tinsulanonda and other government and military notables.

On reaching the Phra Mane Ground, where Their Majesties the King and Queen were waiting in a special pavilion, the urn was transferred to a three-poled palanquin. It was then taken three times counterclockwise around the Golden Meru pyre. Also forming part of the entourage were four Brahman priests dressed entirely in white. As a sign of taking up the aesthetic life, Brahmans do not cut their hair, which they normally tie in a top-knot. Here it was left flowing down their backs as a sign of mourning.

The urn was placed on a barge-like throne and raised into the Golden Meru by means of a pulley device and curtains were drawn across while the golden urn was removed and replaced by the one of sandalwood which would be burned.

In the late afternoon, King Bhumibol and Queen Sirikit entered the Golden Meru to pay their last respects, followed by other members of the Royal Family and long lines of dignitaries all bearing the final offering of paper flowers traditional to the occasion.

When the line of mourners finally came to an end, night had fallen and the spotlit crematorium stood like an image from a fairy tale against the backdrop of the Grand Palace and Temple of the Emerald Buddha.

Later in the night when the public had paid their respects, the King and Queen came once more to the Phra Mane Ground and set a torch to the pyre. Inside the urn was a metal container in which the body of the Rambhai Bharni was cremated by indirect heat.

The following day the remains and ashes of the late queen were collected and three more days of religious rites followed before they were taken to their final resting place – alongside the ashes of her late husband at the base of the presiding Buddha image in Ratchabophit Temple.

It was the culmination of a remarkable display of the links with tradition that still serve as a cohesive force in Thailand's social structure. Respect for ancestors, the dynasty and the past had been duly celebrated.

THAI FANS

Several years ago, in the days before most of Bangkok, including city taxis, was air-conditioned, THAI used to present its passengers with a folding fan with a purple tassel as a souvenir of their flight. A practical little gift, it was also an appropriate token of appreciation being, in its own way, as characteristic of Thailand as the orchids the airline now offers its passengers.

Historically, fans have featured in Thai life and culture to an uncommon degree. From a simple cooling device to royal and religious ceremonial regalia, the Thai fan has taken so many different forms and been fashioned out of such diverse materials as to give it a significance far greater than might be imagined of such a seemingly ordinary item.

Even as once commonplace household objects, used for fanning charcoal cooking fires, as well as for cooling the body, ordinary fans could be enormously varied. Typically, the most basic type was cut from the outer covering of the areca palm or, more attractively, made out of palmyra leaves.

Beyond these humble varieties, personal fans were woven out of split bamboo or certain kinds of grasses and fashioned into various shapes, the most favoured being the pentagon. Alternatively, they might have been made out of feathers, best of all being peacock plumes, in either round or half-circle forms, or shaped like the leaf of the Bo tree.

There were also folding fans, although interestingly always less popular than the single fixed blade variety. They usually consisted of a framework of small pieces of wood covered with paper or fabric but sometimes there were made entirely of thin strips of sandalwood so as to produce a pleasing aroma as well as a cooling breeze.

Although the personal fan is no longer a fashion statement or a functional accessory in today's comfortably cooled world (although past usage is reflected in the not uncommon sight of people flapping a folded newspaper or an invitation card when air-conditioning systems prove insufficient), certain types of Thai fan do retain a traditional role. These are the royal and religious ceremonial fans that the visitor is most likely to see in museum collections, such as in The National Museum or Suan Pakkard Palace in Bangkok.

But although these elaborate flag-like creations make exhibits of genuine value in traditional arts and crafts displays, ceremonial fans are by no means mere relics and are still used in the ritual gatherings of Buddhist monks, as well as on certain regal occasions and represent an intriguing link with the past. Distinctive with their long handles and variously shaped flat (occasionally concaved) blades, ranging from broad, pointed leaf patterns to square or oval forms, these fans are as eye-catching as they are fascinating in their functions.

In royal usage, the fan was most famously featured during the Ayutthaya period at a ceremony known as *Lai Nam*, when the King would wave it towards the sea in a symbolic gesture to the spirits to make the flood waters recede. Later, in the early Rattanakosin (Bangkok) era, such a fan, made of gilded palmyra leaves, became part of the Royal Regalia and today is still seen at some formal court ceremonies, when two attendants stand on either side of the King's throne each holding a fan and periodically turning the long handle with a practised flick of the wrist.

Also surviving from the past is another type of ceremonial fan, the *talapat*, which is used by Buddhist monks during ritual prayers. Exactly when such fans were introduced to Thailand is unknown but it was probably an early influence from the Sri Lankan school and a bronze bas relief dated between the 11th and 13th centuries depicts the Lord Buddha holding a small circular fan while preaching to his parents.

The function of the *talapat* is as obscure as its origins, as no monk is ever seen fanning himself with it. Among various theories as to its usage, the most probable is that the fan serves to obscure a monk's face so that the congregation is not distracted by his appearance.

Whatever its precise traditions and practical functions, the ceremonial religious fan eventually became a kind of regalia signifying a monk's rank and by the Rattanakosin era it was the custom for kings to present what is known as a *talapat phat yot* to monks of distinction, different grades being represented by the fan's shape, ranging from an oval to lotus, flame and cluster shapes.

Not denoting rank but still a ceremonial fan, are the *talapat phat rong*, which are presented to monks by ordinary worshippers at ceremonies held to celebrate special events, such as auspicious birthdays or the blessing of a new house or office.

Besides the two main types of *talapat*, certain fans have an historic value in being created to celebrate important occasions. For example, the 10,000th day of the reign of King Rama V was marked by two specially designed sets of fans, one displaying the royal seals and another showing the various emblems of the government ministries.

Whether as symbols of rank, commemorative objects or simply gifts from worshippers, all monks' fans in the past displayed considerable artistry and care in their design. King Rama IV, for example, is said to have expressed displeasure at one kind of *talapat* that was concave in shape and slightly resembled a serving spoon, the similarity with such a common object he felt was inappropriate. The King accordingly designed a new flat-shaped fan made of bamboo spokes covered with silk or other fabric.

Subsequently, in the latter half of the 19th and the first part of the 20th century, ceremonial fans showed a high degree of craftsmanship in both their production techniques, from woodcarving and metalworking to embroidery, and in their designs, which could be extremely elaborate and colourful, depicting all manner of images from flowers and animals to purely abstract patterns.

Still in use today, the *talapat*, are now not so intricate in design or as imaginative in decoration as those seen in museum collections but they continue to maintain a link with the long custom of fan-making. A minor art perhaps, yet one that in Thailand has an enormously rich and varied tradition.

KNOCKING ON
HEAVEN'S DOOR

The Chinese told the time by it; Japanese geishas used it to compute the cost of their client's entertainment; the Thais thought it a cure for the common cold. Incense has served many remarkable purposes, though most of all it is associated with religious devotion throughout Asia. Its subtle, pervasive fragrance fills temples and shrines throughout the continent.

Incense, more than anything else, evokes the spirit of the Orient. The heady scent and lazy curl of its smoke speak of a different place, a different time. The custom of burning incense has by no means been limited to the Far East but the practice was from early times so widespread as to capture the imagination of travellers, prompting them to refer to Buddhist temples as 'Houses of Incense' and monks as 'Perfumed Kings'.

Burning for a matter of minutes or for days, incense comes in all shapes and sizes. Commonly seen in Hong Kong are huge cone-shaped coils; popular at Chinese festivities in Thailand, Malaysia and Singapore are poles as thick as tree trunks, while simple slender little sticks are found everywhere. Whatever the favoured form, incense remains as widespread as ever in Asia and the daily act of lighting the fragrant substance is so ubiquitous as to transcend ritual and symbolize a whole way of life.

The practice of burning aromatic woods or resins as an integral part of religious devotion or supplication appears to have been common to many cultures stretching far back in time. 'The spreading of the smoke and fragrance of incense,' writes one commentator, 'and the visible movement of that smoke upwards towards the heavens has given it a symbolic relationship with prayer, making the offering synonymous with worship.'

The precise origins of incense are lost in the mists of antiquity, although it was most probably not indigenous to the cultures with which it is so closely associated today. Most informed opinion holds that incense was first used by the ancient civilizations of the Middle East. It was made from the resin obtained from trees of the genus *Boswellia*, plentiful in southern Arabia and Somalia, and the Sumerians and Babylonians burned the substance in the belief it could appease their gods and purify their temples. In Egypt, where incense was used as early as the XVIII Dynasty, the *Egyptian Book of the Dead*, the first known written record of religious and magical ceremonies, notes the burning of fragrant substances as playing a significant part in funeral rites.

With the rise of trade, early Western civilizations came to know and use incense, and Arabian realms such as Sheba, Hadramaout and Qataban made their fortunes from aromatic exports. The Ancient Greek dramatist Sophocles wrote in the opening lines of *Oedipus*, 'the town... heavy with a mingled burden of sounds and smells, of groans and hymns and incense.' In Rome, Nero is said to have ordered the equivalent of a year's production of Arabian incense to be burnt at the funeral of his wife Poppea.

But while incense occurred widely in the ancient world, it was in the Orient that it really took hold, lending definition to whole cultures. Whether the custom spread from the Middle East to the rest of Asia, as some theories claim, or whether it was an independent development, is unknown. What is certain is that the ritual burning of sandalwood was practised in India since earliest times and in China where Taoist text make reference to the use of incense.

From India the substance became established throughout

South-East Asia in tandem with the spread of Buddhism. Initially frankincense and myrrh, the most prized aromatic resins in the Middle East (witness the gifts of the Magi to the infant Jesus), were used in the Far East, mostly imported from Arabia. Gradually, however, a host of other ingredients were employed by incense-makers, including sandalwood, ambergris, basil, benzoin, camphor, clove, jasmine, musk and patchouli.

Illustrating the popularity and ritualistic significance of incense are whole books devoted to various recipes. One Japanese writer on the subject, for example, collected and named no less than 130 varieties of mixed incense. Often recipes would become closely-guarded secrets and families of incense-makers could earn high regard for their own specially devised formulas, described openly only in vague terms – 'a mixture of scented woods and Thai Jasmines', as a Bangkok company defines its particular brand.

The quality of incense varies enormously and depends precisely on which ingredients are used. The basic component of incense paste is sawdust, to which are added the fairly constant ingredients of resins, sandalwood shavings, plant oils and aromatic herbs. For the more expensive, more exclusive products there is a near endless variety of other additives drawn from the whole gamut of natural fragrances.

India is credited with producing today's finest quality incense and its subtly blended fragrances are exported to many parts of the world. China, on the other hand, is the biggest producer, turning out millions of sticks and coils in all sizes. But these two countries by no means have a monopoly and incense-making is widespread throughout South-East Asia, where a long-established cottage industry continues to thrive, unaffected by economic trends or technological change.

Most incense businesses are small family affairs and typically follow the traditional Chinese method of colouring incense with a dye and adding a resin binding agent which hardens when it dries.

Taking a bundle of bamboo slivers, workers dip and dust the ends of the sticks in the mixture, then leave them to dry in the sun, the splayed bunches looking like stranded sea anemones. Incense coils, on the other hand, are made by squeezing the paste through holes in a metal plate to produce noodle-like strands.

Both incense sticks and coils can be small or large. The most common sticks are about 20 centimetres (eight inches) long and burn for an hour or so but there are also sticks as huge as rockets, painted bright red, which will smoulder away for the duration of the three-day Chinese New Year or other protracted festivals. Often these monster incense sticks are brightly decorated with coloured paper, painted dragons and other motifs which lend a striking festive appearance.

Becoming most firmly rooted in Asian cultures through the spread of Buddhism, burning aromatic resins is typically associated with religious practice, Buddhist and otherwise. Yet the precise significance of incense and the way in which it is used can vary widely, as can the purposes, both spiritual and practical, to which it has been put.

An essential component in virtually all Oriental religious offerings, incense can be found from Singapore to Shanghai, from Bangkok to Bangalore. It is seen in all Buddhist temples where fragrant smoke spirals up from countless sticks placed in front of the presiding Buddha image. The same evocative picture is encountered at Hindu shrines and spirit houses honouring all manner of potent forces. The incense is constant, the ritual of its use, however, is complex and varied.

Although it accompanies offerings, incense is not strictly a gift to the gods. It may be considered an end in itself by some cultures but according to widely-held Chinese belief it serves as a conduit for communication, a telephone almost, between man and the divine powers. The gesture of lighting incense engages the conversation; when the stick is consumed, contact with the other world is broken.

Similarly, incense presented with food offerings is not part of the gift; rather the smoke serves as a signal to the gods that a meal has been prepared for them.

Such communication is governed by certain protocol. For example, most gods should be contacted by red-tipped incense but vegetarian divinities are correctly addressed by yellow sticks, spirits via green ones. The number of sticks is also significant. When Thais, for instance, pay homage to the Buddha three sticks of incense are lit but only one is used when ancestors are being honoured.

Such rules vary from culture to culture and between rituals, whether devotional, placatory, celebratory or festive. There is also considerable difference in how incense is burned. Sticks may simply be stuck in a bowl of sand, or consumed in elegant incense-burners, such as those crafted in the past by the Chinese in the form of hills and mountains from which incense smoke wafted like mist.

The finer details may escape the casual observer but today, as in the past, burning incense at religious and festive events throughout Asia captivates the traveller's senses.

Equally intriguing, though now largely forgotten, are the non-liturgical uses to which incense has been put through the ages. Among the more amazing of China's many inventions was the incense clock, which existed as early as the Tang dynasty (618–907 AD). The first fragrant timepieces were in the form of circular wooden seals, about 33 centimetres (13 inches) in diameter and 2.5 centimetres (one inch) thick. The seal was divided into 12 interconnected segments, each representing one *shih*, the Chinese hour which is equivalent to two Western hours. Within each segment was a maze-like path which marked the *shih*'s subdivision, the *ko*, equivalent to 30 Western minutes.

Wood ash was packed into these the interconnecting lines so that when the seal was lifted the pattern remained. A groove was then cut along the full length of the wood-ash path and into this was carefully poured an incense mixture so blended as to have a uniform rate of combustion. When lit the incense would burn along the path at a predictable rate, lasting for a period of 12 *shih*, or 24 hours.

It seems probable that the first alarm clocks also used incense. A 17th-century Jesuit priest recorded how a small weight was attached to the incense at a point calculated to be the desired hour. When the fire reached the mark, the weight would fall, clattering into a copper basin placed under it and so the noise would wake the sleeper.

A variation on the idea was to have a stick of incense prepared with the very last part made of a much more pungent fragrance than the rest. The different, stronger smell, so it was said, would wake anyone having a nap.

The advent of mechanical clocks in the 16th century marked the general demise of incense timepieces; however, it was only in 1924 that incense clocks disappeared from Japan's geisha houses. Here they had been used to measure the minutes a geisha spent with her client.

More prosaic uses of incense in olden times include driving away mosquitoes and other bothersome insects, relieving nasal congestion with a medicinal herb mixed with the incense and simply providing a pleasant aroma in the homes of the well-to-do.

In the past such popularity supported a rich trade in prized fragrances and a thriving industry producing incense in all its full variety. Today the value of the business may have declined but not the use of the end product. Throughout Asia incense smoke continues to spiral heavenwards, providing a vital link between man and his gods and a connecting thread in the enduring cultural fabric of the Orient.

GOLD

'No country has a greater reputation of being rich in mines than the country of Siam, and the great quantity of idols and other craft works which are there seen, evinces that they have been better cultivated there in former times, than now they are. 'Tis believed likewise that they thence extracted that great quantity of gold, wherewith their superstition has adorned not only their almost innumerable idols, but the wainscot and roofs of their temples.'

Monsieur de la Loubère, French envoy to the Kingdom of Siam in 1687–88, was one of the most perceptive and accurate of the early foreign travellers who chronicled what is now Thailand. In this description, from his *A New Historical Relation of the Kingdom of Siam*, he talks with his eyes. In one sense Thailand has little gold and there are scarcely any productive gold mines. In terms of the presence and use of the metal, however, the country is extraordinarily rich in gold.

As La Loubère points out, gold and gilded Buddha images abound and golden ornamentation figures large in the decorative arts for which the Thais have an uncanny skill. In the form of gold leaf, the metal is integral both to decoration and to acts of devotion. In the form of necklaces and other jewellery, it has also long been the favoured form of securing one's wealth and hedging against inflation.

Even if a visitor to Bangkok limits sightseeing to only the most famous landmarks, it is impossible not to discover gold. The golden spires of Wat Phra Keo, the nation's most revered Buddhist temple; the huge gilded chedi of the Golden Mount; Wat Traimit, Temple of the Golden Buddha, with its three-metre (10-foot) high, 5.5-ton image of approximately 75 per cent gold (incidentally the largest surviving example of its kind) – all are 'must-see' attractions.

A slightly less cursory tour will yield sights of devotees placing gold leaf on Buddha images as an act of merit-making, of wooden cabinets and panels beautifully decorated with lacquered designs worked in gold leaf, of countless gilded statues and ubiquitous temple roofs whose golden eaves and finials sparkle in the morning sunlight. Should the visitor stroll through Bangkok's Chinatown, he'll witness a mini gold rush as the district's numerous gold shops enjoy brisk sales every day, regardless of the state of the economy. Typically with red and white counters and their wares garishly displayed in neon-lit, mirror-backed showcases, these shops appear as irresistible Aladdin's caves.

Since man first discovered the bright, shiny metal some 6,000 years ago, gold has been a symbol of purity and wealth. This is as true for Thai culture as for any other. Indeed, in some ways it is more pronounced here than in other societies. Enduring devotion to Buddhism and the monarchy, the two most vital factors binding the society throughout its history, coupled with the Thais innate love of bright decoration, have meant that gold has been profusely used in the adornment of temples and palaces. Popularly perceived as the most valuable and purest metal, it is the most appropriate gift to show respect.

While this is most noticeable in the honouring of the nation's underpinning institutions, it also operates on the everyday level. The Thais, and especially Thai-Chinese, have a tradition of giving gold as wedding presents, as New Year gifts and as valued tokens on similar important occasions. People also buy it for themselves and gold has historically been the most popular form of investment. The attraction of the precious metal has not dimmed today and despite modern opportunities for securing wealth, those gold shops of Chinatown continue to do a roaring trade. As an old Thai saying has it; 'If you have money, you are counted as one's younger brother, if you have gold then you are an older brother.'

Typically bought in the form of chains and jewellery, gold is avidly purchased whenever one has a little spare cash. At the end of the month after salaries have been paid, you'll see young office girls browsing around the counters of gold shops selecting a chain necklace or bracelet. The jewellery looks good but more than anything, the buyers know that unlike the fast-changing fashion scene, gold never goes out of style – nor loses its value.

To show respect and to secure wealth are not the only uses of gold in Thai society. As a substance esteemed for its purity, it is also believed to be effective in placating the spirits. Although Buddhism is devoutly followed by the vast majority of the population, animism was practised long before the national religion was adopted in the 13th century and traces of belief in the spirit world not only persist but provide an existential basis for virtually all Thai customs.

For example, it is a practice among rural communities to place gold leaf in the wooden support poles of elevated Thai houses. This is done to pacify female spirits inhabiting the wood and hence strengthen it. Gold leaf is also put on the prows of boats and other means of transport, since another female spirit, *Mae Ya Nang*, is believed to guard over people on the move. There are numerous such spirits and offerings of gold can help ensure they do not work against you.

The use of gold in what is now Thailand likely pre-dates Sukhothai, the first Thai kingdom, founded in the 13th century. Buddha statues from that period have been discovered with gold leaf clinging to them and some historians claim the custom of covering images with gold came from India prior to the birth of Sukhothai. Others hold that the practice was introduced by Chinese immigrants during the 14th century.

Unfortunately, very few gold artefacts have survived from Sukhothai times and it is not until the second Thai kingdom, Ayutthaya (founded AD 1350), that there is evidence of the precious metal's extensive use. According to one historical source, King U

Thong, the founding monarch of Ayutthaya, had more than 10 halls filled with gold.

Increasingly throughout its 400-year history, Ayutthaya offered an enormous market for gold as the adornment of the city's palaces, temples and countless Buddha images was such as to make it the richest and most magnificent metropolis in the Orient. In its 17th-century heyday, European travellers compared it favourably with the London and Paris of the day. Sadly the city was looted and destroyed by the Burmese in 1767 and historians are left only guessing at the real wealth that was the glory of Ayutthaya.

A few gold masterpieces, such as the statue at Wat Traimit, survived the Burmese invasion by having their true material masked by a stucco coating. The richest single find discovered at Ayutthaya itself, however, is a treasure trove of gold royal artefacts found in the crypt of Wat Rajapurana. Today on display in Ayutthaya's museum, these precious objects include jewellery, royal regalia, containers, votive plaques and Buddha images, all in gold and many set with gemstones.

Undoubtedly gold was an important commodity during Ayutthaya times. La Loubère was probably correct in suggesting that whatever Thai gold mines existed had been 'better cultivated' in the past, though King Narai of Ayutthaya (reigned 1658–88) makes clear mention of the precious metal in his ultimately ill-fated negotiations with the French.

'The various mines are most important for the benefit to the kingdom of Siam and allied countries,' he wrote in a letter of instructions given to a diplomatic mission to the Court of King Louis XIV at Versailles. 'Doubtless the mines not only abound in gold, but are easy to mine. Some areas have already yielded so much gold that we have been able to ship 46 caskets of gold to France. These test mines are of great importance in determining the amount of profit to be gained should mining be carried out in them. You should request His Majesty the King of France to graciously send to Siam the top experts in gold mine operations.'

The death of King Narai in 1688 and the subsequent expulsion of the French from Siam effectively put paid to these plans. Wide, though very thin, gold deposits do exist in Prachin Buri and other parts of the country and these have been worked sporadically. Few mining operations, however, have been commercially successful. Writing in 1912, W.A. Graham mentioned that the majority of prospectors 'invariably met with complete disappointment and, having burnt their fingers, returned to less inspiring but more profitable avocations.'

Today, as demand soars in the wake of the country's burgeoning jewellery industry, Thailand meets its gold requirements, as it largely did in the past, with imports currently amounting to several billion baht annually (not to mention the estimated 10 tons of gold smuggled into Thailand each year). Not all that glitters is new, however. True to its durability and lasting value, gold is frequently recycled, sold back to goldsmiths who re-work it into new chains and other jewellery.

Browsing around the gold shops of Bangkok's Chinatown, you may well be tempted to buy – and why not? It's a good investment. Nevertheless you should know that the local trading weight is the baht, equivalent to 15.16 grammes. Purity of the metal is about 96.5 per cent, or 23 carats, and though this is difficult to prove, buyers rely on the trustworthiness of the shop. If that sounds a trifle risky, just notice the volume of trade being conducted and you'll realize that all of the people can't be fooled all of the time. Trust is the name of the game.

Marvelling at the nation's golden treasures seen in profusion at major sights and monuments, and shopping in Chinatown are not the only attractions of gold in Thailand. Perhaps most fascinating of all is the making and use of gold leaf. This is a traditional craft and one still very much in demand as gold leaf is central to acts of Buddhist devotion. It is placed on Buddha images as a mark of respect and is always sold along with incense, flowers and candles at temples and shrines for use as daily offerings.

Available in little postage stamp-size booklets, gold leaf is remarkable both for its enduring use in religious practice and for the amazing qualities of the metal it illustrates. Gold is heavy yet it is also highly malleable and, in a laborious hammering process, one gram can be turned into 180 square centimetres (28 square inches) of gold leaf with a thickness of 0.0000125 centimetres (1/200,000 of an inch). Incredibly, gold in this form does not crumble and remains whole. Indeed, custom dictates that the leaf must not be split when making an offering.

The fascinating process of making gold leaf can be witnessed at workshops in Bangkok on the Thonburi side of the river. Watching this time-honoured, painstaking craft affords a vivid insight into both the qualities of gold itself and its lasting significance in Thai culture.

The making of gold leaf in Bangkok survives as one of the very few cottage industries in an otherwise increasingly high-tech metropolis. Little appears to have changed over the years and the set-up is basic. A granite block in a backyard serves as an anvil on either side of which stand a pair of beaters, wielding huge hammers. They sit on wooden boards fixed to springy split-bamboo supports, somewhat like car springs, which rock and so aid the beaters' rhythmic action.

The raw material for gold leaf production is imported gold which has been rolled to about the thickness of stiff art paper. It is cut into squares of one centimetre (a third of an inch) which are then sandwiched between pieces of *khoi* (a shrub fibre) paper, powdered and waxed to prevent the gold from sticking. A stack of several hundred of these gold 'sandwiches' are placed in a square pouch made of ox hide.

Professional gold beaters are generally muscular young fellows, commonly stripped to the waist both to allow freedom of movement and in deference to the heat. Firstly, they secure the pouch containing the gold on to the granite block, locking it into a wooden frame by means of two retaining rods – to ensure an even pounding, it is vital the gold squares do not move and slip askew during the hammering.

Then, taking up a 7 kg (15½ lb)-bronze-headed hammer, two beaters start to pound the pouch with alternate strikes, beginning with slow, steadying blows and gradually building up to a firm rhythm. It is punishing work and the beaters generally labour only during the relative cool of the morning.

Between three to four hours of hammering are necessary to complete one pouch of gold leaf. At the end of that time what started out as a centimetre square (a third of an inch square) has been flattened to a flimsy, glittering circle about seven or eight centimetres (2¾ to 3 inches) in diameter.

These rough circles of gold leaf now pass from the brawn of the beaters to the delicate hands of young girls. Using split-bamboo 'knives' and resting the gold leaf on cloth pads, the girls slice up squares of 2.5 centimetres (one inch). If a corner turns over or a fragment breaks off, it is deftly tapped back into place with the flat side of the 'knife' to make each square perfect and avoid wastage. The finished pieces are laid between folds of waxed paper and stacked in booklets ready for sale.

If beating gold leaf takes sweat and muscle, making up the finished squares requires an amazing lightness of touch. The gold is so thin that it will cling to anything if you are not careful and the slightest breath of air sends it flying. A trained girl can turn out up to a thousand squares a day – but if you have neither the experience nor the dexterity you'll find it almost impossible to control the infuriatingly flimsy material.

Appropriate to a most potent offering, gold leaf is the product of strength and patience.

THE
FESTIVE WORLD

Thais love a festival. It's the perfect occasion for giving full expression to the national trait of sanuk, *which means 'having fun', although any English translation inevitably falls short. Of the many festivities punctuating the calendar,* Songkran, *the Thai New Year, and* Loy Krathong *are the biggest national affairs, while* Bun Bang Fai, The Rocket Festival, *best celebrated in the north-eastern town of Yasothon, is one of the most thrilling regional events.*

A WET NEW YEAR

Most of us get to celebrate only one New Year in any 12-month period; the Thais rejoice at three. December 31/January 1 is much as everywhere else, one night of revelry; Chinese New Year, although not a national holiday, is widely celebrated largely as a family affair, but the traditional Thai New Year, Songkran, is a riotous nationwide celebration that involves everyone, locals and visitors, for three days between April 13 to 15 and even up to a week in traditional festive hot spots such as the northern city of Chiang Mai.

Indeed, it is impossible to miss it. In every city, town and village around the country Thais, especially the young, celebrate Songkran in a glorious riot of splashing water over everyone within range. Originally, this would take the form of a respectful sprinkling of water flicked from a silver bowl over passersby, whom would respond with an equally respectful greeting of *Sawasdee Pi Mai*, 'Happy New Year'. Modern times, however, demand modern means and silver bowls have been replaced by plastic buckets, high-power water pistols and, to take the weapons analogy further, 'tanks' in the shape of pick-up trucks carry huge tubs full of water sprayed from a stirrup pump. When you add to this the national trait of *sanuk*, an irresistible sense of fun, you have all the makings of a true carnival atmosphere.

With Thailand's ever-growing popularity as a tourist destination, Songkran has become a major attraction. This is especially so among young budget travellers and every April their favourite hang-outs, such as Bangkok's Khao San Road, turn into Songkran battlegrounds for a good natured mêlée of drenching and high jinks. And this being

Thailand's most popular annual festival, next day's newspapers carry photos of the action with Thais and foreigners alike, all soaked to the skin and smeared with powder called *din sor pong*, in hilarious and boisterous exchanges of water shots.

Although it may not be immediately apparent to the visitor, there is a profound spiritual content to Songkran that runs far deeper than the fun and games. Thailand has adhered to the international calendar since 1941, yet has retained the celebration of the Solar New Year, Songkran. The name is derived from Sanskrit and refers to the movement of astrological bodies, in this case the sun's passage into Aries, the first sign in the Zodiac cycle. Strictly, this would be a movable feast but for modern convenience New Year's Day has been set at April 13, with the celebrations continuing over the following two days.

The origins of Songkran date back to the ancient Hindu culture of India, specifically the spring festival of *Holi*, although parallels can be found in many of the world's cultures, such as, in the West, the old pagan rites of spring, or the Christian celebration of Easter. At the core of all these festivals is the idea of a new beginning, a time of revitalization and cleansing. More specifically to Thailand, Songkran, coming towards the end of the six-month dry season, further serves to invoke the monsoon rains without which the coming agricultural planting season cannot begin.

Since earliest times, water has played a central role in Thai culture, both in practical terms, such as sustaining wet rice cultivation, the principal form of agricultural production, and in symbolic and ritualistic ways as a means of purification and of paying respect. Nowhere is this more readily witnessed than in the various ceremonies that attend the celebration of Songkran. Most notably, Buddha images are paraded and ritualistically bathed in lustral water, while in private ceremonies parents, grandparents, older relatives and teachers are honoured by younger family members respectfully pouring perfumed water over their hands.

Such practices are deeply rooted in Thai custom, but the origins of Songkran's most characteristic display of splashing water over one and all are less clear. Quite possibly it harks back to the ancient belief that the *nagas*, mythical serpents, brought on rain by spouting water from the seas. The more they spouted, the more rain there would be. Thus the Thais demonstrate through the celebration of Songkran that there is water in abundance, so encouraging the forces of nature that control the rains to be equally bountiful.

Also central to the celebration of Songkran is the religious practice of making merit. The most popular way of doing this is by giving offerings to the monks. Of course, this can be and is done on any day, but it is considered particularly auspicious to do so during Songkran as the amount of merit accrued at this time is thought to be greater. Thus on the morning of April 13 people flock to temples bringing a seemingly endless flow of food and other offerings.

Another form of merit-making is to release live birds and fish. The latter custom dates back to the days when Thailand's central plains were flooded during the rainy season. After the water subsided, young fish were trapped in the small remaining pools and the farmers would keep these until releasing them into canals and rivers during Songkran.

On the social side, Songkran also incorporates something akin to the rites of spring and old-fashioned courting games are still played by some village youths. In one such game, girls and boys sit opposite each other and take turns in balancing a wooden disc on one foot while hopping around trying to knock down a similar piece of wood stood on edge in front of a person of the opposite sex. Whatever the outcome – and marriages have resulted – the game is an excellent excuse for teasing and flirting.

Like most traditional Thai festivals, Songkran presents a field day for anthropologists, such being the variety and complexity of the rites and customs. But equally Thai festivals are about having fun, celebrating a good time with enormous verve and passion. Songrkan is no exception; indeed it captures the quintessence of the Thai festive spirit.

Very much a family and community affair (you only have to witness the mass exodus of migrant workers from Bangkok's Hualampong railway station and the long-distance bus stations on New Year's Eve), Songkran is most authentically experienced in upcountry villages. However, for pageantry, parades, music, dancing and 'Miss Songkran' beauty contests, as well as sheer numbers, Chiang Mai is the place to be.

But wherever you are in the Kingdom, you'll find Songkran a festival celebrated as only the Thais know how. It is not always for the faint-hearted, though as one guidebook so aptly advises, 'Hide out in your room or expect to be soaked; the latter is a lot more fun.'

FULL MOON ENCHANTMENT

With the scent of incense filling the night air and myriad candle flames mirrored in the still water beneath the soft glow of a full moon, Loy Krathong captivates the imagination like no other Thai festival.

Celebrated on the night of the full moon of the 12th lunar month (usually late October or early November), Loy Krathong sees Thais throughout the country gather by rivers, canals and ponds to pay homage to Mae Khongkha, goddess of waterways. Kneeling at the water's edge, they launch little lotus-shaped 'boats' bearing offerings of flowers, a candle, incense and a coin both as a gesture of thanks for the gift of water and as a symbolic sending away of ill fortune.

In Thai, *loy* means 'to float', and *krathong* translates as 'leaf cup', which is the focal point of the festival's celebration. The latter is most commonly made out of banana leaves and is something far more elaborate than a mere 'cup'. Frequently it is fashioned in the shape of a bird or a boat and many intricate models, large and small, can be seen in markets and on street stalls in the days leading up to the festival. To see the biggest you need to go to Chiang Mai or parts of the north-east where the people prepare giant community *krathongs*, exquisitely decorated and looking like floral floats in some fantastical flower festival.

(As a variation, the festival is celebrated in a few parts of the country, mostly the North, with hot-air paper balloons rather than *krathongs*, floated up into the sky instead of on water.)

Although the preparation of *krathongs* is elaborate and the festival is extraordinarily popular, attracting Thais of all ages and from all walks of life, Loy Krathong is nonetheless a completely secular affair. It is all a matter of *sanuk*, having fun, enjoying a good time, and there is nothing in the way of ritual or ceremonial involved. You simply light the candle and incense and gently push your *krathong* out onto the water and watch it float away. However, the fact that a coin is placed in the *krathong*, along with the act of lighting a candle and incense, indicate that a deeper cult significance was implied at one time. But the festival's precise origin is obscure and its meaning variously interpreted.

In upcountry districts older members of the farming communities will say that Loy Krathong is an act of remission to the Mother of Water. Their explanation being that in spite of the goddess's bountiful gift of water, man sometimes pollutes rivers and streams and therefore it is only right that he should ask forgiveness.

Alternatively, a religious interpretation is given in a story that tells of how the Lord Buddha implanted his footprint on the sandy shore of the Nammada River of the Deccan at the request of a *naga* (mythical snake), who wished for some image of the Lord Buddha to worship after he had gone. Such a mythical explanation may have helped preserve the tradition of Loy Krathong but it has no basis in the Buddhist scriptures.

Other explanations are found in various folktales specific to different parts of Thailand. Regardless of beliefs, however, the Thais are traditionally an agricultural people whose livelihood depended on the abundance of rain, thus a celebration that pays respect to water while allowing time to enjoy oneself at leisure amid pleasant surroundings provides a fitting pause in the agricultural cycle. With the arrival of the 12th lunar month the arduous task of planting rice from dawn to dusk during the preceding three months is at last finished. Now there is comparative ease as farmers have only to wait until the crop ripens in a month or two. Also the weather is fair after the rains, the sky becomes bright and clear, making it the ideal time for feasts and festivals, for *sanuk*.

101

The idea of sheer enjoyment was stressed by one of Thailand's greatest monarchs, King Chulalongkorn, Rama V (1868–1910), who recorded in *The King's Ceremonies During the Twelve Months of the Year* that Loy Krathong has nothing to do with any recognized ceremony or rite. It is simply a matter of rejoicing in which all people take part and is concerned with neither Buddhist nor Brahman ritual. He added that the festival was connected with the floating lanterns as observed by the rulers of Sukhothai, the first Thai kingdom, some 700 years ago.

Indeed, it is with a romantic legend about Sukhothai that most people associate Loy Krathong and the manner in which the festival is now celebrated. According to the story, there was at the royal court of Sukhothai's King Ramkamhaeng (c1279–98) a beautiful young lady named Nang Nopphamas, the daughter of a Brahman priest. One year, in the 12th lunar month, she witnessed the king and his courtiers picnicking by boat on the city's canals as part of the celebration of Mae Khongkha. However, with her knowledge of Brahman rituals, she felt the Thai ceremony lacked a certain touch of beauty and enchantment.

Thus, with great skill Nang Nopphamas crafted a *krathong* in the shape of an exquisite lotus flower. After lighting candles and incense, she floated this charming gift towards King Ramkamhaeng who graciously accepted it. And so was born the symbol that has ever since marked the celebration of Loy Krathong. In more romantic versions of the legend the king falls in love with Nang Nopphamas and marries her.

It has to be said that there is no historical basis for the story but it is far too romantic for it to be easily dismissed in popular imagination. Today, many of the bigger Loy Krathong ceremonies will have a beauty contest to chose a Nang Nopphamas to preside over the festivities. And the festival is still especially magical amid the ruins of Sukhothai. Here, against the dramatic backdrop of towering chedis and other monuments to the glory of the former capital, thousands throng the banks of the ceremonial ponds to float *krathongs* in the haunting moon-cast shadows.

But no matter where you celebrate Loy Krathong – at a water-front terrace of one of Bangkok's deluxe riverside hotels or by the village stream of an upcountry community – you'll experience a scene of spellbinding charm as moonlight plays hypnotically and timelessly on the water's placid surface and flickering *krathongs* drift slowly away banishing bad luck into the darkness.

ROCKETS FOR RAIN

It's unbearably hot. By 9.30 in the morning the glaring sun is already high in the sky, promising another day with temperatures pushing 37°C (100°F). You can't help wishing the heavens would open up with a cooling shower.

The light brown earth of the paddies is parched and baked hard from the long months of the dry season. Here in Thailand's economically depressed north-east region, a semi-arid plateau that supports only subsistence rice cultivation, it is easy to imagine farmers praying that rains come in time for the new planting.

And that's what they are doing. Each year near the middle of May, villages throughout the area hold a time-honoured festival, staging elaborate rocket-firing ceremonies to placate Phraya Thaen, the sky god, and to remind him of human needs. The biggest and best celebration is at Yasothon, a provincial capital of some 35,000 inhabitants located 580 km (360 miles) north-east of Bangkok.

Yaosthon's annual rocket festival is called *Boon Bong Fai*, which literally means 'the merit of bamboo rockets'. Most Thais are Buddhist, and the concept of religious merit, which is achieved by performing ceremonial deeds, is crucial to Buddhism. But *Boon Bong Fai* is also influenced by traces of ancient animism. Ritualized rocketry is used to appease the spirit world and reinforce the social and psychological structure of traditional rural life. Organized by local authorities and combining parades, beauty contests, holiday celebrations and ritual, the rocket festival ties the themes of fertility, the generative forces of nature, sexual union and rejuvenation into what is basically a rain-invoking ceremony.

These days, the people of Yasothon see *Boon Bong Fai* less as a religious rain-making ritual and more as a time for unbridled fun. As is the case with Mardi Gras, the festival's purgative intent is fulfilled through ritualized license. Social norms are suspended and drinking, flirting and jesting are sanctioned for the occasion.

All the dancing and merry-making revolves around the rocket, the festival's central motif. Yasothon rockets, the direct, if distant, forerunners of today's solid-fuel boosters, range from 1.2 to 4 m (4 to 13 feet) long, excluding their tails. They are packed with up to 40 kg (90 pounds) of black powder to produce a burn time of 40 seconds or more. In the Middle Ages, when the ancient Chinese art of rocketry was exported to the West, these rockets would have been state-of-the-art.

On this sweltering Sunday the people of Yasothon are amassing at a little park on the edge of town. Some are mere spectators, out to enjoy one of the most eagerly awaited festivals in the regional calendar; others, mostly young men, are uninhibited revellers, wildly costumed and fantastically daubed with paint and mud. They dance and prance about in high spirits – literally in many cases; bottles of potent rice whiskey are freely passed from hand to hand.

Some of these exuberant local lads carry very big homemade rockets. The largest has a 4-m (13-foot) body and a 10-m (33-foot) stabilizing tail, and six men are needed to bring it to a cluster of rickety wooden launch platforms at the side of the park. Each platform is about 11 m (35 feet high) and angled skyward at around 80 degrees.

For a moment, attention shifts to the clearing in front of the platforms, where a troupe of 60 or so colourfully attired young women begins a folk dance in honour of the sky god. Their slow, rhythmic movements are accompanied by drums, cymbals and gongs.

Then the first rocket goes up with a deep roar and a trail of billowing smoke. It soars high and straight – a good omen in the eyes of the enthusiastic crowd. The rest of the day will be punctuated by the launching of rocket after rocket, just to make sure Phraya Thaen gets the message.

The day before, a parade down Yasothon's main street had featured more than 20 floats. The celebrants transformed utilitarian trucks into glorious chariots: a huge, lavishly styled model rocket was the centrepiece of each float, while the truck's hood took the form of a *naga*, a mythical snake figure and water symbol. Enormous cut-out figures of characters from the *Ramakien*, Thailand's national epic, adorned each vehicle's sides. A few real rockets also made an appearance, accompanied by the young men who made them.

The parade wasn't scheduled to start until 12.30 but by early morning the ferris wheels on the fairground were running at capacity. Loudspeakers were blaring Thai music and vendors were hawking fresh fruit, dried squid and brightly coloured iced drinks.

In the early afternoon, after the governor of Yasothon wound up his opening address, the fun began. Thirty or so *talai* rockets – bamboo hoops with rockets angled across the diameter – provided a spectacular start. About the size of Frisbees, the rockets are launched similarly, with a flick of the wrist. With exaggerated nonchalance a reveller would light the fuse with a cigarette, hold the hoop loosely until the very moment of ignition, then toss it away. Each rocket made a few horizontal spins before soaring to several hundred feet with a tremendous screech.

The parade started to roll. Floats alternated with groups of young dancers performing traditional local dances. Themes of agriculture, fishing and rural pastimes predominated. Interspersed throughout were bands of pranksters, some riding on trucks with their own high-decibel sound systems, others mingling with the crowd. All were dressed outlandishly: one man wore a long red skirt with black trim and looked for all the world like a flamenco dancer; a tall, slim guy in cowboy gear coolly strutted about like some small-town Western sheriff; a blackened half-naked warrior sucked on a tube that ran over his shoulder to a bottle of rice whiskey tucked into his hip pocket; and, prompting appreciative laughter from the crowd, a tubby fellow paraded about in green paint and a frog mask. Many splashed each other with paint or mud.

But for the rocketeers, the highlight of the weekend is Sunday's contest. The competition is divided into three size categories ('small' is defined as under two metres (six and a half feet) in length and 15 cm (six inches) in diameter). There is prize money to be won, but that doesn't cover the cost of most rockets – which can easily take up to 20 days of painstaking preparation – and everyone in each rocket team chips in for the expenses.

Rocket casings were originally made of bamboo but in the recent past most contestants changed to metal pipe, which is strong and convenient – but dangerous if it explodes. In 1984 a bystander was killed by flying shrapnel from a metal rocket. Now the organizing authorities urge the use of plastic pipe: it's safer and lighter than metal, and rocketeers reinforce the interior with zinc sheeting and tightly bind the outside with cord or steel wire to limit fragmentation. Still, a few old-timers bemoan its relative weakness.

Even so, a plastic tube makes quite an effective rocket once it has been packed with fuel. The desired blend is 10 parts saltpeter, which acts as an oxidizer, and three parts carbon in the form of homemade soft-wood charcoal. The saltpeter is dissolved in hot water before the carbon is added, and each batch is tested in short rockets before being put into service.

Team members pack the powder into their rockets a batch at a time, tamping it down with a wooden ramrod. The most difficult part of the procedure is boring a hollow central core through the powder for the exhaust gases. This job, performed with a pointed or corkscrew-tipped rod, requires an expert's touch. The core must narrow gradually toward the top and be perfectly straight, with no blockages or unduly wide cavities. Any mistakes will cause the rocket to explode on the launch pad.

The top and bottom of the tube are then plugged with a mixture of clay and sugar – the latter acting as a binding agent – and capped with wooden plugs, which are bolted to the body. The rocketeers can now connect long, slow-burning fuses, sometimes with firecrackers attached, to the base of their missiles. The fuses are made of rope or strips of saffron-coloured cloth that look as if they were torn from the discarded robes of Buddhist monks. Maybe there is some propitious quality in this, although ignition failure is the most common problem at *Boon Bong Fai*. Finally, the rockets are fitted with long bamboo tails to stabilize their flight. These are attached about two-thirds of the way up the casing and bound at several points.

As the teams ready the rockets, making last-minute adjustments and re-affixing fuses, huddles of gamblers bet on the rockets' flights, while pranksters, in accordance with tradition, throw rocket makers into specially created mud pools.

The smaller rockets are set off first, and it is not until the afternoon that the few four-metre (13-foot) monsters take to the air. One, two, sometimes all three launch pads are used at once, though the long erratic fuses prevent many simultaneous launches. With much swaggering – and staggering – the teams set up their rockets and, as in a game of chicken, the most drunken member usually lingers, clinging to the frame and leaping clear only seconds before the fuse catches.

Some rockets fail to ignite, others blow up on the launch pad, but the really good ones may reach 300 or 600 m (1,000 or 2,000 feet). Since there is no instrument for measuring altitude, the contest is judged on ground-to-ground flight time. The winning time is usually around 50 seconds, although the record stands at 70 seconds.

The last rocket isn't fired until after five o'clock. Later that night, the roar of the rockets still ringing in the revellers' ears, rain clouds gather over the region.

THE
NATURAL WORLD

Originally an agrarian people dependent on wet rice cultivation, the Thais have traditionally lived close to nature. Water, for example, is a recurring feature in the social and cultural fabric. Still today there is much, from sacred plants to the inside-out concept of domestic architecture, which remains as a reminder of a harmony with and respect for nature.

THE LOTUS

For more than 5,000 years, the lotus has captivated man's imagination. To the ancient Egyptians it was a symbol of Nerfertem, the personification of the sun, believed to burst forth each day from a lotus. The flower was also identified with the Egyptian god Horus, ruler of the sky. But most of all, it is throughout Asia that the lotus has been praised for its delicate beauty and revered as a sacred symbol of goodness. Growing in profusion and widely featured in daily life and ritual, it blooms with an emotive power unmatched by any other flower in the entire continent.

To most Asians the lotus symbolizes fertility and purity – clear associations with two of the plant's most notable characteristics, rapid growth and exquisite beauty. In India, the lotus has been identified with Lakshmi, the wife of Vishnu and a form of the Mother Goddess. A similar association with fertility is found in Japan, where the lotus flower or stalk is popularly believed to promote human fecundity.

The generative force of the lotus is also noted in a graphic incident recounted in the *Mahabharata*. This ancient Indian epic describes the god Brahma as having sprung forth from a lotus that grew out of the navel of Vishnu when the deity was reclining in sleep, absorbed in the dream of the universe.

It is Buddhism, however, which makes the most widespread use of the lotus as a symbol, and the flower serves as one of the four fundamental emblems of the faith, along with the Bo tree, the wheel of law and the *chedi*. Like the Lord Buddha, the lotus is born in an impure world from which it strives to free itself. Its roots are buried deep in mud and the plant germinates in the murky depths of pools and ponds. But, thrusting its stem high above the surface of the water, it blossoms in the pure sunlight.

As a recurring image, the lotus appears in countless Buddhist myths and legends, most famously as blossoms which miraculously opened under the feet of the new-born Prince Siddhartha, the Buddha-to-be, as he took his first steps on earth.

In Thailand, the persistence of the lotus motif is vividly seen today at the little canal-side village of Bang Plee, just outside Bangkok, where the end of Buddhist Lent is celebrated by showering a huge Buddha image with thousands of lotus buds. At the highlight of what is known as the annual 'Receiving of the Lotus' festival, a huge gilded statue of the Enlightened One is paraded by barge along the village canal. Joyous crowds throng the banks and flowers rain down until only the Buddha's head remains visible above the mounting floral offerings, tokens of the peoples' devotion.

It is an enchanting occasion, celebrated amid a whirl of colour and excitement in which religious devotion is mixed with all the fun of the fair as only the Thais know how. But it is the symbolism of the lotus itself that accounts for the festival's origins.

Before it was settled as a village, Bang Plee stood amid paddy fields where Thai farmers, who lived along the banks of the nearby Chao Phraya river, came every year to plant and harvest rice. Then, in the 19th century, a group of Mon people from Burma settled in the area, and they noticed how the Thai farmers, before returning home, cut lotus flowers to offer to the Buddha. So, the following year, when the farmers came to plant rice again, the Mon lined the banks of the canal at Bang Plee and offered lotus flowers as a gesture of friendship.

Although the flower is widely found in ritual and symbol, its name is more evocative than indicative and the term 'lotus' has since ancient times been applied to several seemingly similar but botanically different water plants. What was a lotus to the ancient Greeks is not the sacred flower of Asians, and Homer's famous lotus-eaters of the Odyssey did not partake of the same flower as that clutched by Thai Buddhists in their devotions.

The flowers eaten by those Greeks belonged to *Zizyphus lotus*, a bush indigenous to southern Europe, and the lotus of Egyptian symbol was a plant akin to the water lily. The sacred flower of the East, however, found from India to China and Japan, is something quite different. In botanical terms it is *Nelumbium nelumbo*, a white- or pink-flowering water plant found exclusively in Asia (a yellow-flowering species occurs in parts of North America).

In spite of a delicate-looking bloom, the Nelumbium lotus is robust and thrives throughout the Asian continent in a huge variety of environments, from temperate to tropical. Although there are certain obvious parallels with the equally prevalent water lily, the lotus is botanically quite distinct. Most noticeably, the leaves do not float on the water like those of the lily, instead they grow from the muddy depths of ponds to rise several centimetres, sometimes a metre of more (a few inches to three feet), above the surface. The flowers, composed of five large petals, shoot up further still to sway majestically at the end of long fibrous stems. After blooming, the lotus produces seeds in a pod distinctively shaped in the form of a flat-topped cone.

Not surprisingly for a plant so readily found, the lotus is put to various practical uses in Asia. It is, for example, eaten, but while the ancient Greeks became forgetful from their brew, the Thais and others in the East take their lotus both as a medicine and as a tooth-some dessert.

A potion made from boiling the roots in water is a traditional medicine for stomach upsets, specifically that of inner heat caused by eating too much durian or longan fruit. More generally lotus roots, which can be eaten raw or cooked, contain an easily digested starch that is particularly suitable for the old or the sick.

For a different more pleasant taste, lotus seeds can be enjoyed raw as a handy snack. Along with melon seeds, they are particularly popular with train and bus travellers, who typically pass the time endlessly peeling the casings and nibbling the slivers of white flesh. The seeds, boiled in syrup, are also used as an ingredient in the characteristically sweet desserts so beloved by the Thais.

Moving away from the flavour of the plant but remaining in the kitchen, the large round leaves of the multi-purpose lotus make ideal disposable mats on which to serve food. Alternatively they may be used as tray liners or for other decorative purposes in the presentation of a meal. Leaves are further used as a wrapping for rice that is then steamed so it becomes fragrant with the subtle aroma of the lotus.

On a more prosaic level, the fibres that can be extracted from lotus stalks make excellent wicks for oil lamps. Then again, there is a cosmetic that is derived from dried flower stamens, and even a love potion made from the pollen.

The uses to which the lotus has been put by various Asian cultures are as numerous as they are diverse, yet the flower is remarkable for nothing so much as its beauty. It may be a common-or-garden plant, found as often in a muddy roadside ditch as in an ornamental pond, it has nonetheless been an unfailing source of inspiration for philosophers, poets, writers and artists.

Most visible of all is the lotus motif in art. A prolific ornamental form in various cultures, stylized lotus shapes have appeared as capitals and other architectural decoration since the time of the Assyrians. In the Far East, a unique use of the decorative form is found in the lotus-bud *chedi* created in the 14th century by the Thais at Sukhothai.

Here, Wat Mahathat, the largest temple complex at this ancient city, is distinguished by a *chedi* which follows the traditional pattern of a tapering tower rising from a tiered base, except it has a bulbous finial in the shape of a gracefully curved lotus bud. No mere whimsy, the form became an established architectural feature of the age, helping to define an evolving Thai aesthetic.

The lotus-bud *chedi* of Sukhothai's Wat Mahathat is but the most dramatic example of a motif widely seen in all kinds of Buddhist art.

On temple walls, pediments and columns, in murals and on Buddha images, this sacred flower forms a recurring pattern running through the religious fabric of Thailand and other Buddhist lands. Painted blossoms and leaves often form the background to colourful murals; thrusting lotus stems are carved in wood, stone and stucco; frequently the very image of the Buddha rests upon a lotus pedestal, and should the Buddha be shown seated cross-legged in meditation, the pose is known as the 'lotus position'.

In written form the lotus assumes more sensuous connotations, and a Sanskrit love poem claims: 'Your eyes are two lotus buds,/Your hand, the full-blown flower,/Your arms, its gracious roots.'

The last word on this exotic flower of the Orient perhaps best belongs to the 11th-century Confucian scholar Chou Tun-yi. To him the lotus symbolized a human ideal: 'How untarnished as it rises from its bed of mud!' he wrote in a famous passage once taught in Chinese schools. 'How modestly it bathes in the clear pond. It is unobstructed within and straight without... it stands upright gracefully. It is good to behold from a distance but it tolerates no intimacy.'

THE SACRED TREE

The Bo tree haunts the Buddhist world with the impact of a surrealist painting. Its long twisting aerial roots penetrate walls, snake over rocks, entwine buildings and wrap themselves around Buddha images to form dramatic sinuous frames. Old trees in temple compounds have their heavy drooping branches supported by props like a melting form in a Daliesque landscape. Gaily coloured strips of cloth knotted around the boughs and trunk add a painterly effect.

Bo tree, Bodhi tree, Banyan, Pipal, call it what you will, *Ficus religiosa* is a potent symbol in Thailand and throughout Asia. It is one of a huge number of species of trees and shrubs that comprise the ficus genus.

Some are small and prosaic, like the fig tree; others are huge and haunting. In Calcutta's botanical gardens there is a famous *Ficus bengalensis* that is reputedly more than 200 years old and has some one thousand aerial roots which look more like the trunks of separate trees. Less spectacular but with their own mysterious power are two Bo trees at the forest cave temple of Wat Tham Sua in southern Thailand. Soaring to a great height, their trunks are seemingly supported by flat buttress-like aerial roots as tall as an elephant.

Its strange form suggesting a sense of primordial power, the Bo tree has been venerated from earliest times. Certain aboriginal peoples of India are known to have made festive offerings to it, while it later came to be revered by the Hindus. But it was the advent of Buddhism that elevated the tree to its most sacred status.

In the 6th century BC the Indian prince Siddhartha achieved

enlightenment as he sat under a Bo tree at Bodhgaya, and thus attained Buddhahood. Since no images of the Buddha were made until several hundred years after his death, followers of the religion he founded held the tree as sacred and took it as one of the three most recognizable symbols of the faith. (The other two are the Wheel of Law and a crouching deer which represents the first sermon in the deer park at Sarnath.)

Even after Buddha statues began to be sculpted from the 1st century AD onwards, the tree and, in particular, its heart-shaped leaf retained a symbolic value. Devotees may make a talisman of a leaf that has been inscribed and blessed by an especially revered monk. It also forms a recurring pattern and, for example, the *sima* boundary stones around a Thai Buddhist temple's holiest building are fashioned in a leaf shape. So, too, are the clappers in the tiny tinkling temple bells of Thailand and Myanmar. In China the leaf was a popular motif in early Ming porcelain, while the tree itself is found in Chinese cave paintings and in the temple murals of Thailand, Myanmar and Sri Lanka which traditionally depict scenes from the Buddha's life.

The original Bo tree under which the Buddha achieved enlightenment was, according to legend, poisoned by a queen of Emperor Ashoka. He was a devout Buddhist convert but the jealous queen felt he spent too much time praying beneath the tree's branches and so brought about its destruction. A reputed direct descendant, however, survives at Anuradhapura in Sri Lanka, the land where the religion received fresh impetus after its expulsion from India. This tree continues to be venerated as one of Sri Lanka's most important Buddhist relics.

While not the original, a sacred Bo tree still shades the holy site at Bodhgaya where the Buddha meditated and saplings from it are considered special. Bangkok's famous Wat Benchamabopit, popularly known as the Marble Temple, has one such illustrious offspring.

This lineage is distinguished but not essential as all *Ficus religiosa* are sacred to Buddhists. No devotee would ever willingly destroy a

Bo tree, at least certainly not before an elaborate ceremony has been performed to prevent the ill fortune that would surely result from such an act. And despite the tree possessing little practical value, it is allowed to spread its roots at will.

Entangled among sacred ruins or shading temple compounds and with the strangeness of its physical attributes perhaps enhanced by Buddha statues around its base, the Bo tree presents some of most evocative images of Buddhist Asia.

WATERWORLD

'The existence of the people of Bangkok may be called amphibious', wrote Sir John Bowring, Queen Victoria's envoy to Thailand in the 1850s. 'The highways of Bangkok are not streets or roads, but the river and the canals. Boats are the universal means of conveyance and communication...The children pass much of their time in the water, paddling and diving and swimming, as if it were their native element.'

More than the fabulous temples and other exotic sights it was the widespread presence of water that initially struck foreign travellers to the Siamese Kingdom. Writing some 300 years before Bowring and describing not Bangkok but its predecessor, Ayutthaya, a Portuguese Jesuit noted that the city was 'like Venice because one travels more by water than one does by land. I've heard it be said that there were over 200,000 boats, both large and small. I do not know if there are 200,000 boats but I did see a league's length of waterway which was so full that one could not pass.'

The fact of the matter is that the Thais are an essentially amphibious people. Not that they have been great seafarers (in the 17th-century heyday of seaborne trade most of the business was conducted by Muslims and Chinese) but the Thais are lowland people who have always been water oriented. The country's long coastline gave rise to fishing communities, although more central to the rise of Thai civilization was the pattern of settlement in river valleys and on flood plains.

Indeed, rivers have played a crucial role in the development of South-East Asian civilizations. With wet rice cultivation as the people's staple support, populations grew up in the valleys, basins and delta areas of the region's major waterways. Water made the lands fertile and further provided transportation links. Moreover, inland riverine settlements were less open to attack and more easily defended than coastal towns. Basically, whoever held the river valleys ruled.

Such a pattern of valley settlement is made vividly clear by the example of northern Thailand, a mountainous area divided north to south by four main rivers, the Ping, Wang, Yom and Nan. It was not by coincidence that the ancient northern kingdom of Lanna rose to power only after securing the broadest of these valleys, the Ping at Chiang Mai. Here it was able to consolidate a power base and exert control over the entire region.

The development pattern of the dominant central Thai civilization was similar. The four rivers of the North meet up near Nakhon Sawan to form the Chao Phraya, the country's principal waterway in terms of size and significance. On its banks were founded both Ayutthaya, the nation's capital for over 400 years until its destruction in 1767, and its successor Bangkok, which was bestowed with capital status in 1782.

These were not just riverside towns, they were island cities. Ayutthaya was sited at the junction of the Chao Phraya and two tributaries, while the core of Bangkok was located on a broad bend in the river turned into an island by the cutting of an artificial channel. In both cities natural waterways were augmented by numerous connecting canals.

In was perhaps inevitable that early European visitors would dub Ayutthaya and, later, Bangkok 'Venice of the East', travellers having a tendency to make such glib – and often exaggerated – comparisons. Yet in the case of Ayutthaya, the soubriquet referred to something more than a fancied similarity, and was firmly based on the fact of the city's watery nature.

For the 17th-century French missionary Nicolas Gervaise the position of the Siamese capital 'is finer than that of Venice, even though the buildings are less magnificent, for the canals which are formed by the branches of the river are very long, very straight and deep enough to carry the largest vessels.'

The practical advantages of a waterborne city were manifold. Rivers and canals facilitated transport in and around Ayutthaya, while the Chao Phraya itself served as the main communication link with the outside world, allowing ocean-going ships to reach the capital but, at the same time, permitting easy control of that shipping and so avoiding any surprise attack. Waterways also supported the population of Ayutthaya by irrigating the paddy fields and hence ensuring plentiful rice harvests.

What was true of the capital was reflected throughout the Thai countryside. The physical make-up of Thailand's Central Plains is such that much of the area used to be inundated for a month or two every year. The land is low-lying and level, thus causing rivers to divide into numerous channels and creeks which, with the total absence of roads in former times, lead to water being the principal means of commerce and communication. Thus, towns and villages, if not developed as full island settlements like Ayutthaya, were always constructed facing rivers and canals. Homes were built on stilts, being amphibious in the sense that they could stand equally on land and in shallow water, and the people went to market travelling mostly by boat.

The same principles of secure settlement were adhered to when Bangkok became the capital. Initially after the fall of the Ayutthaya, Thonburi, located on the west bank of the Chao Phraya opposite from Bangkok proper, was the nation's interim power centre. That changed when King Rama I ascended the throne in 1782 and decided to move the capital across the river. The main reason for this was strategic; Bangkok could be made a readily defensible island city by linking with canals the northern and southern ends of a broad westward curve in the river. This original core of the capital, the site of the Grand Palace and other major classical buildings, is still referred to as Ratanakosin Island.

The pervasiveness of water in traditional Thailand was such that its presence and use were not limited to the practical, to defence, transportation and irrigation, but also to leisure and ritual. Those same early travellers who commented on Ayutthaya's physical resemblance to Venice, further remarked that the most pleasant excursions and the grandest processions took place by boat.

The recreational function of water received similar attention when Bangkok was created. In reference to the digging of one of the new capital's main canals in the 1780s, the *Dynastic Chronicles* record: '[King Rama I] wanted it to be a place where the people of the capital could go boating and singing and reciting poems during the high-water season just like the custom observed in the former capital of Ayutthaya.'

Not until the mid-19th century did Bangkok begin to build its first roads suitable for wheeled traffic and even in the early 20th century writer W.A. Graham could still talk of a waterborne culture. 'The rivers and canals are the arteries of nearly all the traffic of the country and are continually thronged with innumerable boats and vessels of many descriptions,' Graham remarked in his 1912 book *Siam*. 'Notwithstanding the recently-constructed railways, 80 per cent of the produce of the country is carried by water to the markets, while the various journeys and errands which take people abroad upon the roads in other countries are here all performed in boats... The Siamese children learn to swim almost before they can walk, and the whole population is familiar from earliest youth with the management of boats of all kinds.'

Life on the water may not be quite so vibrant today, but waterborne traffic remains greater than might be imagined. Remarkable though it may seem considering the inordinate number of cars in Bangkok, the Chao Phraya is still a significant highway, used by many people who commute daily to central Bangkok from Thonburi on the west bank and from the northern suburb of Nonthaburi.

Serving this traffic are Chao Phraya express ferry boats that criss-cross the river, picking up and dropping off passengers at the score or so of landing stages on both banks. Other smaller craft ply a simple back and forth ferry service at various points, while travellers in a hurry can hire a longtail boat, a sleek craft powered by a huge outboard engine that speeds across the water sending out a wake that rocks more somnolent river-users.

Ferries and longtail boats do not have the river to themselves. The Chao Phraya retains something of its old importance as a link between Bangkok and upcountry provinces and continues to serve longhaul transportation. Trucking by road is now the most common means of moving bulky produce, though the river can still be an economical alternative and strings of huge black iron barges can be seen navigating a slow majestic path through the bustle of small craft at Bangkok.

With produce as well as passengers being transported by water it is scarcely surprising that rivers and canals should have been, and remain to some extent, market places. Norwegian traveller Carl Bock described the Chao Phraya as he saw it in the late-19th century as 'a sort of aquatic Covent Garden market, where dozens of small skiffs are floating about, "manned" by one or two women...disposing of their fruit and vegetables, their firewood, and varied up-country produce.' Such activity continues today and the so-called 'Floating Market' is a priority Bangkok sight even now.

Indeed, many of Bangkok's prime historic sights can still be glimpsed by cruising the river. Besides major monuments like the Grand Palace, numerous old buildings line the river banks. Interesting sights just in the stretch between the Mandarin Oriental Hotel and Wat Po include the French and Portuguese embassies – two of the city's oldest foreign missions; the former Customs House; the classic Chinese-style Wang Lee House; Santa Cruz Church; Wat Arun and lesser known temples like Wat Kalayanimit, and old royal residences such as Chakrabongse House, built by a son of King Rama V.

Nor is it just history that can be gleaned from cruising the waterways. The banks of the river on the outskirts of Bangkok and the side canals yield scenes of traditional riverine lifestyles that have scarcely changed over the years – little wooden houses built high on stilts front the water's edge, youngsters splash about in their aquatic front yards, girls bathe demurely in their sarongs, men fish lazily from sampans. It is all part of an amazing water world.

Just as water has been a pervasive physical presence in the development of Thai civilization, so has it served a symbolic role that runs through the cultural fabric like a silver thread. This is best summed up by the Thai word for river, *mae nam*, which literally translates as 'mother water' and suggests both the nurturing value of the primal element and the respect it thus commands.

When coupled with Buddhism, the national religion, water, both sustaining and transparent, becomes a symbol for the spiritual support and purity of the Buddha's teachings, and lustral water is widely featured in religious blessings and rites of passage. In the traditional Thai wedding ceremony, for example, well-wishers pour water over the hands of the bridal couple, while at life's end the ritual bathing of the dead is an integral part of the funeral rites.

Water is also widely associated with the practice of serenity and meditation, in which mental clarity and a fresh lucid mind are symbolically linked to the purity of a river. Moreover, in Buddhist legend, Lord Buddha achieved enlightenment whilst seated under a Bo tree facing a river, and as a reminder of this most temples, especially in rural areas, are constructed facing a river or a canal.

Nor is it too fanciful to imagine that, for people whose lives were traditionally spent close to rivers and canals, a placid nature and graceful, fluid movement (most readily witnessed in Thai classical dance) have drawn influence from the quiet, easy flow of water.

TRADITIONAL THAI HOUSES

With Bangkok's high-rise building boom peaking in the mid-1990s, traditional Thai teakwood houses retain a precarious foothold on the urban landscape and only showcase properties, such as the Jim Thompson House, are readily seen by the visitor. The builder's craft survives, however, and workshops near Ayutthaya offer a fascinating glimpse into an enduring tradition.

At the tiny village of Hua Hat roofs of traditional Thai houses, their unmistakable curved eaves rising elegantly to pointed peaks, can be seen standing by the side of the highway. The view is a far cry from the tranquil canal-side setting once typical of Thai homes but these wooden buildings are not here to stay. They are the products, soon to be sold, of half-a-dozen small workshops where craftsmen carry on a tradition of house-building largely unchanged since the days when Ayutthaya was the capital of old Siam.

That these workshops should exist in an historic yet now scarcely residential district illustrates immediately a vital distinction of Thai-style houses. They are essentially portable. In the past when people moved house, they did literally that. Posts and panels would be carted off and reassembled at a new site, a task that could be accomplished in a single day with the help of neighbours.

As prefabricated structures Thai houses have walls made of movable panels that are assembled on site, attached to a framework of sturdy columns and beams. Typically, the walls slope slightly inward, which enhances the graceful look, although it results from support pillars being fractionally angled to prevent subsidence. Holding everything together are wooden pegs. Non-wooden elements were, and still are, so rare in traditional Thai houses that Joseph Conrad, describing Bangkok in the late-19th century, could remark, 'in these miles of human habitation there was probably not half a dozen pounds of nails.'

Roofs, covered with either wooden or ceramic tiles, are steeply sloped and given a broad overhang to provide protection from the bright sunlight and torrential monsoon rains. There may also be a second, stepped roof level to give ventilation.

Then the whole structure rests on stilts to raise it a couple of metres off the ground and afford protection from floods, snakes and other wild animals, as well as to facilitate air circulation. In former times, this ground floor space also provided convenient stabling for the family's livestock.

Traditional Thai domestic architecture draws a less distinct line between outside and inside than do homes in cooler climates, and completing the basic design is a verandah. This is an integral element in a dwelling where some 40 per cent of the space is intentionally set aside for outdoor living. Apart from affording a shady spot for escaping the worst heat of the day, the verandah can be turned into a kitchen garden with potted plants.

Given their prefabricated form, Thai-style houses may be simple or complex. The essential unit is a rectangle some 3.5 by 9 m (12 by 30 feet), allowing space for one or two rooms, but the living area can be easily enlarged with the addition of further units. As many as eight or 10 components, arranged around a central platform, can be integrated to produce one large dwelling sufficient to accommodate the extended family, as was the custom in the past.

Big or small, Thai houses all follow the same construction principles; principles that are preserved by today's craftsmen. 'It all begins with the roof,' explained Mr Sommai who runs one of Hua Hat's six carpentry workshops. 'Not only is the house size dictated by the roof's dimensions, the whole beauty of the structure stems from the line of the roof. If a mistake is made in the curve, then all the rest of the house will look wrong.' That is all the more remarkable when blueprints are not used and Sommai, like other house-builders, has to trust to his own eye.

Although he admits to using some modern tools – a saw bench, electric sanders, etc – Sommai says he works according to the old ways that he learnt from his father, a carpenter for 50 years. To illustrate the point, he shows a wall section in the making, its several variously sized panels all perfectly joined by the time-honoured tongue-and-groove method, reinforced by wooden pegs.

Also having learnt from the past is Mrs Samruay Sae Nim, owner of a well-known factory producing traditional homes located on the Ayutthaya-Ang Tong road. 'By buying and selling old houses,' she remarked, 'I learnt the basic principles of house-building that have been followed since ancient times.'

She discovered the most important guidelines to follow are how wide and how tall the structure should be. But initially she was baffled to find old houses do not follow precise measurements; one section might be, for example, three metres, 10 centimetres (12 feet, 4 inches) instead of three metres (12 feet) exactly. Then she realized carpenters in the past did not cut wood to size; it was all a matter of eye and experience. This accounts for a building's individual character and the fact that no two houses are exactly alike.

Although all Thai houses are based on the same principles, each province has its own subtle variations. 'The most beautiful houses come from Suphanburi and Ayutthaya,' Mrs Samruay said. 'They are taller, more graceful and have more harmony.' Indeed, harmony is very much the key to the aesthetic appeal of Thai style. But architecture must also address the functional as well as the aesthetic. Just what is so appealing about the traditional?

'Thai houses have many advantages,' Mrs Samruay confidently claimed. 'They are cooler than modern homes because they have good ventilation and are designed to maximize air circulation. Then the materials are better; teak lasts much longer than concrete and wooden plugs are stronger than nails. Part of the reason why traditional houses have become popular again is because they are better built than their modern counterparts. You won't find any cracks after two or three years.'

Not all agree that a return to the past is a turn for the better. 'Thai houses look nice and romantic but the rooms are quite cramped and dark,' remarked one architect. 'In the past, people just used their rooms for sleeping. Most other activities were done outside the room, on the open verandah or in the space under the house. Thai houses cannot get along with the new lifestyle.'

Yet the flexibility of Thai style can still serve today. 'If you wish to have a Western interior, you can add the ceiling, glass windows, window screens, and install the air-conditioner,' Mrs Samruay said.

There is, however, a modern trend for 'applied' Thai style in which the open space beneath the house is closed in, as with a contemporary home, while the upper storey retains the old-style wooden superstructure. Something of the original harmony is lost in such buildings but they do offer greater possibilities for combining modern living facilities with traditional design.

While the pros and cons of Thai style may be debated by architects, traditional houses are, according to their advocates, more than just teak poles and panels. They are believed not only to be possessed by spirits of their own, they are also thought to be lucky.

ON THE CUTTING EDGE

The table is as pretty as a picture. Serving dishes spread with folded banana leaves set out in geometric patterns brim with roses in full bloom, with chrysanthemum petals unfolding and with sprays of delicately veined leaves. There are also model boats with lace-like sails, fish and other animals, ornamental bowls and traditional betel boxes adorned with geometric patterns drawn from classical Thai art. None, however, is the kind of dinner table decoration you would expect. Look closely and you'll discover the roses are actually tomatoes, the sailboat a papaya with sails of watermelon... everything is carved from fruit and vegetables. It is not so much a case of more than meets the eye, as what meets and dazzles the eye is more to eat.

As attested by countless restaurants around the world, not just in major capitals but also in smaller cities and towns, Thai food has become widely appreciated as one of the truly great culinary arts, and rightly so. Not only are the tastes rich and varied, presentation and eye-appeal are given almost equal importance, hence the craft of fruit and vegetable carving is an integral skill in the Thai chef's accomplishments. Indeed, there is an intricate pattern to the evolution of Thailand's culinary art, and so steeped in tradition is it that it reflects the complex weave of the Kingdom's cultural fabric as a whole.

Long before someone in the West indelicately suggested that the way to a man's heart is via his stomach, Thai women in their wisdom realized that they could charm their husbands by their cooking ability. With polygamy then socially acceptable, culinary creativity was sensibly viewed as a way of keeping a man's respect once physical attractions began to fade. Excellent and varied dishes produced day after day not only pleased a husband but also gave the wife a means of successfully competing with younger, prettier, would-be rivals.

Accordingly, young women were taught before marriage not to rely solely on their physical beauty; culinary skills were crucial. This importance placed on cooking is illustrated by no lesser a person than King Rama II (reigned 1809-24). When a prince at the court of King Rama I, as one account has it, he fell in love with one of his father's nieces, who besides being beautiful, was reputedly an excellent cook. Love blossomed most likely at the dinner table and the prince wrote songs in praise of the variety of the girl's cooking. The romance was eventually fulfilled and the prince and the niece married, the girl in time becoming Somdet Phra Sri Suriyentharaboromarajini, the mother of King Mongkut, Rama IV.

Winning a royal heart through one's culinary skill may seem an extravagant claim but, as one commentator has put it, 'In Thailand food is more than a necessity, it is yet another aspect of everyday life that has been elevated into something of an art form, in which every detail takes on its own special importance.'

The foundation for this art form is, of course, the country itself. Thailand is especially blessed by nature and the bounty of the land is quite staggering. Not only is some of the finest-quality rice grown here, there is also a huge variety of vegetables, fruit and spices which thrive in the fertile soil. So cooks have at their disposal an unusually wide selection of fresh ingredients.

That is but the beginning. How Thai chefs take advantage of the land's bounty is indicative of a culture in which time is perceived more freely than in the West and in which principles found in other Thai arts – concern with harmony and visual impact, for example – are all given full play.

Time is of the essence, but in a reverse way to how it is most often perceived in other cultures – slower not quicker. The preparation of a Thai dinner can take all day, starting in the early morning with shopping at the local market for the day's freshest and best buys. Then the spices, essential ingredients of Thai cuisine, must be prepared anew for each meal, painstakingly ground to ensure the perfect blend and the fullest flavour. And so on with each of the several dishes – meat, fish, curries, vegetables, salads, soups – that comprise one meal, each receiving the individual attention it deserves.

In such careful preparation lies one of the secrets of Thai cooking. The food is not, as many foreigners popularly think, spicy hot. Some dishes may set the tonsils afire but generally the key to the distinctive tastes lies in the balance of spices, herbs, roots and leaves intended to enhance the natural flavours and textures of the main ingredients. As well known Thai master chef, Chalie Amatyakul, points out in his book *The Best of Thai Cooking*, 'If one were seeking a single-word summation of Thai food, the word would not be "heat" but "harmony"; a harmony of tastes, colours and textures, designed to appeal to both the eye and the palate.'

Pleasing the palate is, naturally, the aim of any cuisine worthy of the name. Visual appeal is also integral to any great culinary art, although it is perhaps the one facet most often overlooked or poorly executed. Not so with Thai cooking.

Throughout their history the Thais have excelled in the decorative arts, the surface appearance of forms assuming an exceptional importance in the overall concept. A brilliant example of this is traditional temple architecture in which woodcarving, gilt work and coloured glass mosaic among other decorative details put a stunning finish to the building. Elsewhere, decorative genius finds superb, if surprising, expression in food preparation with the art of fruit and vegetable carving.

The practice of carving food items into delicate and intricate patterns, as well as into figurative forms, has a long tradition in Thailand

and its believed origins are, like so much else in the culture, linked with royalty. As legend has it, it was during the Loy Krathong festival in ancient Sukhothai, the first Thai capital, that a lady of the court decorated her *krathong*, a festive offering to the Mother of Waters, with fruit and vegetables carved into an elaborate floral display. The King was so taken by the beauty of the art that he decreed the skill should be taught to other ladies in the royal household.

Indeed, food carving long remained an art practised exclusively by the ladies of the royal court, who would turn cucumbers, papayas, tomatoes, carrots, radishes, onions and other prosaic foods into exquisite works of art fit to decorate a king's banquet table.

In democratic Thailand fruit and vegetable carving spread and became a popular accomplishment in the kitchens of homes at all levels of society, where mothers would pass on the traditional skills to their daughters. Today, with the enormous increase in international recognition of Thai cuisine, the art positively thrives. There have been books and television programmes on the subject and in Bangkok Thais and foreigners alike can take professional courses in the art. Nor is the interest merely academic; classic Thai restaurants place the proper traditional emphasis on food presentation, while buffet spreads at weddings and other gala events commonly make a great show of carved fruit and vegetable displays, which add considerably to the celebratory atmosphere. In such contexts the art is an expression of the Thais' inherent sense of hospitality and respect due to honoured guests.

Essentially, all that is required to turn a common-or-garden tomato or whatever into a bouquet of delicately petalled flowers is simply a small and very sharp pointed knife – plus a good deal of skill and enormous patience. Other implements such as a curved knife, a vegetable peeler and so on may be called into play, although the craft is in the hand and the eye not in the tools. Accordingly, it is essential that the knife is held properly, that is held like a pen near the point. This aids steadiness of hand and also makes it easier to control the depth of the cuts and the uniformity of designs.

The fruit or vegetables to be carved should be at room temperature and, except for tomatoes, immersed for a while in ambient temperature water to help maintain freshness longer. As for the material itself, the fruits and vegetables that lend themselves best to carving are watermelons, pineapples, papayas, cucumbers, radishes, carrots, tomatoes, onions and chillies.

When it comes to the actual carving, the basic skill is understanding the texture of the particular fruit or vegetable, along with appreciating the natural colouring, and seeing how these two factors best lend themselves to imitating any chosen subject. Fine, dense substances permit deeper cuts and hence the possibility for more intricate patterns and forms. Gradations in colour are also possible depending on how deeply the skin is pared away.

Naturally, it takes some training and much practice to master the art of fruit and vegetable carving but a few simple examples should serve to whet the appetite for further study.

A cucumber is one of the easiest vegetables to carve and, for instance, a model rice barge can be made by cutting a slice off the long side, so the cucumber will be stable. Then you mark the upper length into three sections, cut through half the vegetable's thickness and remove the two end sections, leaving the middle portion intact. This leaves you with the shape of a boat with a central canopy. Small v-shape cuts can then be made to decorate the top of the barge, before scooping out the inside of the cucumber.

Another simple form is a tomato tulip: starting from the bottom, cut five equal petals, separate the skin from the pulp and remove the top half of the pulp; finally add a stem made from a spring onion pierced by a flexible stick. Also common is a tomato peel rose: start at the top and peel away the skin plus a thin layer of pulp in one continuous strip about a centimetre (half an inch) wide, then roll the skin around loosely in the shape of a rose, while 'leaves' can be made by cutting a green chilli into four or five strips.

The cynic may well ask why anyone should go to such lengths to transform a tomato into a rose. The answer is the Thai's innate appreciation of beauty and craftsmanship, whatever the medium; and, perhaps, also an understanding that the beauty of a good wife is more than skin deep.

BETTER BANANAS

It is not easy to be serious about a fruit that is variously slang for insane, a staple for slapstick slip-ups and a phallic symbol. Yet my attention was caught recently by a front-page headline in *The Nation* announcing: 'Scientist to engineer a better banana'. If I'd thought about it at all, I would have imagined nature had done a pretty good job with the fruit but no, according to the newspaper report, researchers think they can come up with a disease-resistant variety of the plant.

Rather more remarkable about the story, however, were the statistics it gave: farmers in 120 countries grow an estimated 95 million tonnes of bananas annually and the fruit is the fourth most important crop in Africa and Asia. In fact the banana is the world's most widely consumed fruit, nowhere more so than in Thailand, where just about every part of the plant has its uses, culinary and non-culinary.

Botanically belonging to the genus *Musa*, of the family *Musaceae*, the banana is indigenous to Asia. In his 1883 study *Origin of Cultivated Plants*, Alphonse de Candolle remarked: 'The antiquity and wild character of the banana in Asia are incontestable facts. There are several Sanskrit names. The Greeks, Latins and Arabs have mentioned it as a remarkable fruit... Sages reposed beneath its shade and ate of its fruit.'

Asia's rightful claim to the banana as its own was, however, obscured by the early worldwide propagation of the fruit. Before the Christian era, banana plants were brought from India to ancient Greece and Egypt, while Arab traders introduced the fruit to the Guinea Coast of Africa. It was here, in the 15th century, that Portuguese colonists discovered bananas and found them tasty, fast-growing and easy to transplant. Also on the Guinea Coast, the fruit acquired its English name, derived from the West African word *banena*. From Africa the Portuguese took the banana to the Canary Islands and from there, in the early 16th century, the fruit came to the New World.

Today the banana is grown throughout the world's tropical regions – indeed, the silhouette of its distinctively broad and bent leaves is the very image of the tropics – and intensive cultivation has resulted in more than 100 varieties, of which you can find well over 20 in Thailand. Known locally as *kluay*, the fruit ranges from the long yellow *kluay hom thong* (Gros Michel), one of the most popular commercial types noted for its sweet aromatic flavour, to the finger-sized *kluay khai*, or the *kluay namwa*, another sweet variety familiar to many Thais as a staple of their diet in infancy.

One of the varieties, known locally as *kluay tanee*, is less popular, however, not because of its fruit but because there is a belief that the plant is inhabited by a female spirit, *nang tanee*. This type of banana is therefore never planted near a house lest the spirit bring misfortune; though if properly propitiated she is said to assist in love affairs.

A giant herb and not the small tree it appears, the banana in all its varieties has much to recommend itself as a source of nutrition. Besides its soft flesh, which makes it an ideal baby food, the fruit is rich in potassium, as well as natural sugars that provide energy – note how certain tennis stars these days chomp on a banana between games. Bananas are also recommended as promoting good digestion.

Fully appreciating nature's gift of a nutritional fruit that grows year-round, the Thais have been extraordinarily creative in devising ways in which bananas may be consumed. While most of us simply see a nice plump ripe banana as a dessert, with or without ice cream, the Thais view it as a versatile food that can be used in various forms other than at the peak of ripeness. Young green bananas, for example, are served with a spicy sauce and eaten raw as a vegetable. Slightly more developed, but still not fully ripe, bananas are sliced, sun-dried and fried for a snack.

Indeed, the menu of cooked bananas is extensive; besides the familiar banana fritter (*kluay khaek*), you can have grilled bananas soaked in syrup (*kluay ping*), bananas boiled in coconut milk (*kluay buat chi*) or in syrup (*kluay chuam*), or bananas smoked in their peel (*kluay phao*).

Traditional though the banana is, it has not been overlooked in Thailand's modern development and a number of projects have been launched both to expand the use of the fruit and to provide improved livelihood for farmers. In 1991, the Organic Hom Thong Banana Project was established in Phetchaburi province as a joint Thai-Japanese venture to cultivate toxin-free golden bananas for export to Japan and is currently producing some 50 to 60 tonnes a month.

More recently, in 1999, the Processed Banana Project was begun in Chachoengsao province and is now a widely supported initiative between government agencies and the private sector whereby groups of farmers' wives are assisted in producing and marketing processed products. These include banana chips, banana jam, banana paste and banana jelly.

Besides these joint public and private sector undertakings, various private concerns are engaged in marketing brand name banana products, like the Panwa banana chips in three flavours (paprika, barbecue and cheese), or the Oriental Princess Company's shampoo and conditioner made from *hom thong* bananas. I've also been told of, but not yet had chance to taste, a banana wine developed by the Horticulture Department of Bangkok's Kasetsart University.

As versatile as the banana fruit is as a food item, so have the Thais been versatile in their use of the plant as a whole which, indigenous to the country, is very much a part of the culture. The making of *krathongs*, those little floats in which you sail away your troubles at the Loy Krathong festival, is but one of many examples of how the large, flat banana leaves lend themselves to cutting and folding and fashioning into various forms. Typical are small containers in which to steam and serve food, and wrappers for sweets. The whole leaf – fresh, clean, disposable and biodegradable – is a perfect display base for foodstuffs as commonly seen on market stalls.

In non-culinary uses, banana leaves are said to make soothing dressings for burns and blisters; smoked dried leaves can be rolled into cigarettes, and the tough outer fibres of the stem are used to weave rope. Children have also found ingenious ways of making toys out of the banana plant, most famously in the *ma kan kluay*, a hobby-horse that country kids have traditionally fashioned out of the stiff spine of the leaves. Also, young girls weave rings and necklaces from banana leaves, while boys will use the stem to carve out toy guns. Better bananas indeed.

JUST DESSERTS

Her husband was executed for treason but Lady Phaulkon lived on to spread sweetness throughout the land. It sounds like the improbable end of some trashy historical romance and yet it is literally true.

In the late 17th century, Constantine Phaulkon, a low-born Greek of remarkable character and ability, had risen in the service of Siam to become King Narai's first minister, no foreigner before or since having held such a high position. These were times of political intrigue of Byzantine proportions and Phaulkon, always a controversial figure, eventually fell from grace, a victim of the Revolution of 1688, when the reins of State were seized by the highly-placed courtier Phra Petracha as Narai lay on his deathbed.

Although Phaulkon was arrested, tortured and executed (albeit on dubious charges), his wife, Marie, was spared. Initially harshly treated at the hands of Petracha, who had her viciously flogged in a vain attempt to make her reveal the whereabouts of Phaulkon's supposed treasure hoard, she was eventually given her freedom and put in charge of cooking and education at the royal palace.

It was a position for which Marie was admirably qualified. Of Japanese, Portuguese and Bengali descent, she had a cross-cultural background that had instilled in her a devout Catholic faith along with pronounced domestic skills. Among the latter was an expertise, learnt from her mother, in the culinary arts, most notably in the making of cakes and sweets according to recipes that the Portuguese had brought to Japan.

What was most innovative about Marie's cooking was the Japanese-Portuguese habit of using eggs as the base for a variety of cakes and desserts. The Thais had developed a sweet tooth long before Marie entered the kitchen but never before had eggs featured in their dessert recipes. Hence *foi thong*, *thong yip* and *thong yot* – literally 'golden thread', 'pinched gold' and 'golden drop' – which are essentially confections of egg yolk and syrup, although with different methods of preparation, became culinary novelties at the Royal Court at the end of the 17th century and today remain widely favoured Thai desserts (*khanom*).

Both the continuing popularity of egg-based desserts and their regal association have been highlighted by H.R.H. Princess Maha Chakri Sirindhorn in a charming little cookbook that gives the recipes for nine 'golden' sweets. The fascination is enhanced by the book featuring the nine offspring of one of His Majesty the King's favourite pet dogs, *Thong Daeng*, each of which has been named after one of these very special desserts.

The link between this royally sponsored recipe book and Lady Phaulkon's confections produced for the 17th Court illustrates the regal thread that runs through Thailand's culinary art, including desserts. Both King Rama II and King Rama VI wrote poems about *khanom*, among other food, and it is the former's reign, between 1809 and 1824, that now defines the classic period of royal Thai cuisine, when new creations were devised and old recipes revised. From this time dates one of the most complex Thai *khanom*, called *ja mongkut*, a dessert painstakingly fashioned to look like a fruit and made from wheat flour, egg yolk, coconut milk, sugar, water melon seeds and jasmine flower water.

This all goes to show just how wrong many Thai cookbooks published in English are when they say that the concept of desserts in the Western sense does not exist, and so generally give only scant attention to sweet platters. Yet while it is true that a typical Thai meal is not divided into courses, a variety of communal dishes being served at the same time, sweet things are on the menu and will usually be eaten last.

What is different about Thai desserts is that they are really in a class by themselves, so rich and satisfying that they serve as filling snacks on their own and are as widely found – perhaps more so – among street hawkers' wares as on the dining table. Nor is there any dearth of choice; one well-known two-volume Thai cookbook contains recipes for 58 *khanom*.

Fresh fruit is the most common and simplest way to finish a Thai meal and cleanse the palate – one says 'simplest', although Thailand produces a staggering variety of tropical fruits. From the common-or-garden banana to more exotic delights, such as mangosteen, rambutan, pomelo, or the foul-smelling but delicious-tasting durian, the choice of fruits is virtually a menu in itself.

Fruits, along with rice, especially the glutinous variety, also provide the basic ingredients for the majority of concocted desserts. And just to give an ironic twist to it all, there is a Thai sweet, *luk chub*, which looks like miniature fruits but is actually made of crushed beans dipped in jelly.

Perhaps the most famous of all Thai desserts, certainly one that is eaten with a passion as much by foreigners as by locals, is mango and sticky rice (*khao neow ma-muang*), in which coconut milk, mixed with a little sugar and a pinch of salt, is used as a topping to strips of the fruit. Alas the mango season is short, peaking in March and April, so it is another fruit, the banana (*kluay*), as well as the coconut (*ma-phrao*), that are the basic ingredients for a host of desserts and sweet snacks.

An abundant year-round fruit, bananas loom large in Thai desserts. Boiled banana in coconut syrup (*kluay buat chii*) is often served as an after-dinner sweet treat; this is a warm dish of chunks of the fruit stewed in coconut milk with sugar and little salt added. Bananas may also be grilled over charcoal (*kluay ping*); puréed (*kluay guan*), fried (*kluay kaek*) either sliced and dipped in batter or whole and coated with shredded coconut and flour; steamed in their own leaves (*khanom kluay*), in which the fruit is crushed and mixed with coconut and flour before being moulded and wrapped in leaves ready for steaming; or, for those with a really sweet tooth, boiled in syrup (*kluay chuam*).

As much a dessert staple as bananas, the coconut features not just as a cream topping but also as the ingredient for making Thai custard (*sangkaya*), which thus has a flavour distinctly different from that found in Western recipes. This popular dessert can be eaten plain, with sticky rice or as a filling in the classic pumpkin custard (*sangkaya fuk thong*).

Equally classic is coconut pudding (*khanom krok*), instantly recognizable among street hawkers for its traditional preparation using a round pan with hollows, like a baking tray, in which the batter is poured, then covered and heated over a charcoal stove. Another baked favourite is shredded coconut pudding (*khanom paeng jee*), with ingredients including glutinous rice flour and palm sugar, while both coconut syrup and the fruit's flesh is used in a toothsome dish of tapioca balls *(bua loy sakhuu ma-phrao awn)*.

Other popular desserts include baked mung bean cake (*khanom maw kaeng*); black glutinous rice pudding (*khao neow dam piag*); tapioca balls shaped around pieces of water chestnut, dyed red and served with coconut milk and ice (*thap thim krawb*, which means 'crispy rubies' in reference to the dish's appearance); coffee jelly (*wun ka-fae*); flower-shaped cookies (*khanom dok lamduan*), which come closest to Western style cookies … the list is near endless and the discovery of Thai *khanom* can be a travel experience in itself.

Because generally only the lighter and more dainty sweets are served as a dessert in the Western sense, as the conclusion to a full meal, you need go out onto the street to explore the full range of *khanoms*. Street vendors are ubiquitous and often easily recognizable – there is no mistaking the shouldered twin pot-laden baskets of the seller of tapioca strings in coconut syrup (*khanom plakrinm kai tao*), nor the desserts-on-wheels man with his perspex display case mounted on the back of a three-wheeled pedal cart and stocked with Lady Phaulkon's golden treats.

WE ARE SIAMESE
IF YOU PLEASE

Well, yes, Siamese cats do come from Siam, as Thailand was known before being renamed in 1939, but today you'll see more of these sleek felines sitting proudly on window sills or monopolizing the most comfortable chair in the room in Western homes than in the land of their origin.

Quite simply, due to a lack of dedicated breeders, the number of pure pedigree Siamese cats in Thailand has dwindled drastically over the last hundred years. Conversely in the West, where the Siamese was first introduced in the latter half of the 19th century, its popularity has soared to the extent that it is now probably the world's most instantly recognizable cat breed, its aristocratic demeanour immortalized in the lyric 'We are Siamese if you please, we are Siamese if you don't please' from the Walt Disney cartoon feature *The Lady and the Tramp.*

Assuredly an Eastern cat, the precise origins of the Siamese are unknown and it is possible that this highly individualistic cat was common in many parts of Asia, its mutation occurring more than 500 years ago. The mutation was likely widespread and, as mentioned in Dr Bruce Fogle's *The Encyclopedia of the Cat,* in the late 1700s the naturalist Pallas described a white-bodied cat with dark feet, ears and tail in central Asia.

In Thailand, however, these cats were especially prized, raised as pets by royalty and the aristocracy, as well as by Buddhist monks, the cats winning favour for keeping rodents from nibbling Buddhist manuscripts in the temple libraries.

Although stories about Siamese cats being 'Royal Cats of Siam', protected by royal guards and included in the entourage whenever the Royal Family travelled are by and large exaggerations, the historical importance of the cat in Thai culture is attested by the beautifully illustrated manuscript known as the *Tamra Maew*, 'Cat Poems', and dated to the 17th century.

There are at least eight known versions of the *Tamra Maew*, six housed in Bangkok's National Library, as well as several copies of the now fragile *khoi* paper manuscripts. The vivid paintings accompanying the texts are a sheer delight in themselves, artfully capturing cats in different postures and with different expressions, and while some are fanciful, others are a true record of the cat breeds of the day. In all, the *Tamra Maew* depicts some 17 breeds of Thai cats, recognizable among which are pointed cats that are the ancestors of the Siamese we now know, the copper-coloured *Suphalak Thong Daeng* and the silver-blue *Si Saswat* (Khorat) cat, along with tabbies, bi-colours and spotted cats.

Complementing the illustrations are texts that are both poetic and enlightening on the believed properties of each cat. Thus the green eyes of the *Si Saswat* are likened to the colour of a dewdrop on a lotus leaf and its fur to the silver-grey of a rain cloud (a more welcome sight in tropical Thailand than perhaps in the West).

As for explanations of the cats' properties, all are said to bring luck to their owners, the type of good fortune varying according to the type of cat. For example, the *Suphalak Thong Daeng* (sometimes referred to as a lighter-tone Burmese, although darker 'Burmese' cats were also known in Thailand and were possibly 'Siamese' before being introduced to Burma) is supposed to promise high military rank, while the *Kao Taem*, a white cat with nine black spots, brings luck to traders.

When the *Tamra Maew* was compiled (and its origin, or that of similar manuscripts, could far predate the 17th century provenance of the existing copies as so many records were lost in the 1767 destruction of Ayutthaya), Siam was largely closed to the Western world. There had been contact with major European powers – notably Portugal, Holland, Britain and France – in the 16th and 17th centuries, but the Revolution of 1688 lead to the expulsion of most foreigners and it was not until the mid-19th century that the country again opened up to diplomatic and trade relations with the West. Such long isolation gave rise to the perception of Siam being a secretive and exotic land and the mystique was inevitably attached to Siamese cats when they first appeared in the West in the latter years of the 19th century, brought home by traders and missionaries.

The arrival of these exotic felines, their striking appearance enhanced by the myths of their being 'royal' cats, coincided with the first formal cat show held in 1871 at the Crystal Palace in London. Here they captured the public's imagination, though not all were enamoured and one judge reportedly described them as an 'unnatural, nightmare kind of cat'. Cat fanciers, however, thought otherwise and after British diplomat Owen Gould brought home England's first breeding pair in 1884, the Siamese was embarked on a path to becoming the world's favourite feline.

While the Seal Point, known in Thai as *Wichien Maas* and distinguished by vivid blue eyes, a glossy pale fawn coat and dark seal-brown face, ears, feet and tail, is the most typical Siamese cat, the breed also originally included solid colours, but the incredibly strict breed registration and judging criteria subsequently drawn up by Western breeders and cat associations have relegated these to being 'Oriental Shorthairs'.

Over the years, other colours aside from the classic Seal Point have been bred and vary from blues and lilacs to cream and cinnamon points. Body shapes, too, have changed and for many breeders a wedge-shaped head is preferred over the rounder look of the original imports. It's a matter of opinion how far such designer breeding is to be favoured – personally my four Oriental Shorthairs are as Siamese as I please – but interestingly the pointed cat is not viewed by most Thais as the number one local variety. That status belongs to the *Si Saswat,* or Khorat cat, which was named by King Chulalongkorn, Rama V, after the region in north-eastern Thailand where it is found.

Not only was the *Si Saswat* favoured as a pet by the wealthy, it has for centuries been regarded as greatly auspicious. Most strikingly it is the focus of an odd rain-evoking ceremony traditional to the Phimai district of Nakhon Ratchasima (Khorat) province, where both cat and ceremony are believed to have originated. In the ritual, a *Si Saswat* cat is paraded in a bamboo cage as villagers sprinkle it with water to appease the rain god.

Also widely prized, and a favourite of King Chulalongkorn, who entrusted one of his sons with the task of breeding them, is the *Khao Manee.* This is a pure white Siamese exceptional because of its striking eyes, one of which may be emerald green and the other topaz yellow.

Regardless of breed and pedigree, or lack of it, what is most likely to strike visitors today about Thai cats is that a great many of them have a kink at the end of their tail. The legendary explanation for this (and I've never discovered a factual one) is a Kiplingesque 'just so' story that tells of a princess who before going to bathe in a lake took off her rings and bracelets and threaded them on her cat's tale for safe keeping. However, when the cat swished its tail the jewellery fell off into the lake. So next time the princess went to bathe and took off her rings she tied a knot in the cat's tail so they wouldn't be lost. And that is how Thai cats came to have kinked tails.

THE
ART WORLD

Thailand has a rich tradition of classical art, ranging from the visual arts, such as temple mural painting, to classical dance drama and other performance arts. Much of it is inspired by Buddhism and created primarily to serve the national religion, while the Ramakien *epic tale has further been a huge influence on virtually all art forms.*

A PAINTED MENAGERIE

Animals populate the Thai world in rare abundance and variety. The elephant is emblematic of the nation; the water buffalo is as clichéd a figure in the Thai rural landscape as the Monarch of the Glen is in the Scottish highlands; the fabulous *garuda*, half man and half bird, is the insignia of the Royal Thai Kingdom and appears at the top of official documents; *naga* snakes undulate along the balustrades of temple staircases; lions, monkeys, birds, horses, cats, dogs and other real animals as well as fabulous creatures of the imagination all abound.

Given the myriad roles animals play in Thai life and myth, it is not surprising that they have been favoured subjects among Thai artists. What is remarkable, however, is the consummate skill employed in their depiction. 'The observation is so keen, so powerful the feeling of life,' writes art historian Jean Boisselier, 'that the Thai artists must rank high among animal painters – and this is without any debt to the traditions of China and Japan.'

Nowhere is the truth of this more marvellously apparent than in Thai illustrated manuscripts. The 'books' that were probably produced throughout Thai history present an extraordinarily rich field for the appreciation of Thai classical painting, though an oddly neglected one. Temple mural paintings, partly because they are more readily visible, tend to overshadow manuscript illustrations in spite of their having for the art historian enormous advantages over murals. Manuscripts are generally more easily preserved and, because of this, they have rarely been restored in the way most murals were at various times repainted, regrettably often poorly so.

Like murals, however, illustrated manuscripts have suffered the ravages of time, insects and a tropical climate, while the sacking of Ayutthaya in 1767 was a catastrophe comparable to that of the destruction of Alexandria's famous library in classical times. Accordingly, while the art of manuscript illustration has in all likelihood a long tradition, few examples surviving today predate the 18th century. To judge what must have been lost you only have to look at the 14th-century inscribed stone plaques at Wat Si Chum in Sukhothai. Depicting the birth tales (*Jataka*) of the Buddha, these are superb examples of line drawing, one plaque in particular showing a magnificent horse seated on a cushion, a previous incarnation of the Buddha.

The manuscripts that do survive from the 18th and 19th centuries fulfil the promise of the artist's work at Wat Si Chum, and while the 'books' cover all manner of subjects, from Buddhist cosmology and divination to military treatises, animals are not only widely featured in their illustrations but also arguably the most accomplished elements in the compositions.

Manuscripts are of two types; those written on palm leaf and those on *khoi* paper, made from the bark of a bush. The former were produced by scratching the surface of dried and trimmed palm leaves with a needle, then bringing up the engraved areas with black ink made from soot. These loose-leaf productions were used primarily for religious texts and were little illustrated.

With continuous 'concertina' pages often running to several metres (yards) in length, *khoi* manuscripts were altogether more substantial in content as well as form, being profusely illustrated with pictures that could be both decorative and integral to the texts. There seems to have been no set rule for the placing of illustrations; they can cover a page, a double-page spread or just the centre of a panel, although the later manuscripts generally follow the pattern of pictures running either side of the text. In some cases, however, notably the technical treatises on diverse subjects, the pictures were integrated with the text.

However placed, all illustrations were clearly of great importance and so finely executed that brushes were traditionally made from the inner hair of a cow's ear. Colours, natural pigments mixed with tree sap as a binding agent, are mostly brighter, livelier and more varied than those seen in mural paintings.

What was shared with mural painting was the convention of filling all available space within the picture area, with the result that backgrounds are often as detailed and fascinating as the main subjects. Animals in particular lent themselves to this custom, and it is not unusual to see finer observation and more poetic expression in their depiction as decorative background detail where the artist has given freer reign to his imagination.

The principal subject matter of the manuscripts falls into two broad categories, religious and secular, in both of which animals figure large. The two most popular religious texts were the *Traiphum*, a Buddhist cosmology, and the *Tosachat*, which records the last 10 incarnations of the Buddha. All manner of weird and wonderful creatures populate these mythical worlds and, beside the well-known *gardua* and *nagas*, there are, for example, four species of lion, ten species of precious elephants and seven large fish.

But the mythical forests of the *Traiphum* and the worlds of the Buddha's past lives are not solely inhabited by creatures of the imagination. Deer, tigers, birds and other real-life animals intermingle with the fabulous, showing the artists' powers of observation as equal to their imagination. The postures of cavorting animals is brilliantly captured and the best illustrations manage to be impressive and charming at the same time, imbued with a poetic quality that reinforces the life of the animal kingdom without sinking into sentimentalism.

Although many of the animal illustrations show idyllic worlds, where the charm and gentleness of the creatures are matched by the softness and beauty of flowers, the artists did not ignore the ruthless side of nature. In the same late Ayutthaya period manuscripts in which you see frolicking animals in blissful surroundings you'll also find fierce beasts in duels to the death. In one a panther and a tiger have their teeth buried in each other's hindquarters, the blood flowing. In another picture a tiger is attacking a buffalo, ripping with its teeth and claws while its prey defends itself with its horns.

While religious subjects were dominant in the 18th century, manuscripts of the 19th century were more varied and include treatises on a wide range of topics from military strategy to medicine and the precise arrangement of ceremonial parades. For the animal painter it was a rich field and creatures, either symbolic or decorative, find a place in all manner of subjects. An 1815 military treatise, for example, has a superb illustration of troops deployed in a formation known as 'king-lion', which is set in the figure of a rampant mythical lion.

A more literal rendering of animals is found in a number of manuscripts that serve as manuals on various creatures, most commonly elephants. In these every conceivable aspect of the elephant is defined and mostly illustrated, from the pachyderm's mythical ancestors to technical information on the capturing, training, handling and care of elephants.

Instructional though these manuscripts are, their illustrations are not merely supportive of the texts and in their humour, charm and the uncanny way in which they capture defining characteristics, distinctive postures and grace of movement, they stand as works of art unparalleled in the photography and drawings of today's books.

MYTHICAL CREATURES

Huge birds, monster snakes and fabulous hybrids abound in Thailand. None is to be found in any of the Kingdom's zoos or wildlife sanctuaries, yet all are highly visible. A favoured habitat is the temple compound, while they are also commonly sighted in town where they are recurring symbols attesting to a unique species of fauna.

Despite often fearsome appearances, none of these creatures are harmful. Indeed, most are benign, serving to aid and protect man. They are, of course, all mythical with no corporal being, yet alive in the human mind and given recognition in a menagerie of statuary and ubiquitous motifs.

Every culture has its enduring legends populated by weird and wonderful creatures and Thailand is no exception. In a host of myths and popular beliefs is to be found a rich store of the fabulous, which in the nation's historical development served to underpin and help give meaning to a physical world of uncertain existence.

Top billing in the roster of Thai mythical beings goes to the *garuda*, a powerful creature half bird and half man, and the *naga*, a monster king snake. Popular in both Hindu and Buddhist cosmology they are half-brothers and demi-gods, powerful beings with various roles and hence widely portrayed in Thai art, as well as being favoured symbols serving a variety of roles. Although the father of the *garuda* and *naga* was the same, they had separate mothers, Vinata and Kadru, two sisters ever jealous of each other. It was their mutual animosity that gave rise to their respective offspring becoming sworn enemies. Differing stories recount the origin of the enmity.

According to one tale, the two sisters once had a bet on the colour of the Sun god's horse; Vinata said it was pure white while Kadru claimed it had black hair mixed with white. Afraid of being wrong, Kadru had her thousand *naga* children change themselves into strands of black hair and cover the horse's body. Thus she won the bet by a cunning trick and Vinata became her slave with resulting ill-will.

Another legend tells that while Kadru hatched a thousand eggs which became *nagas*, Vinata had only two offspring, one becoming the *garuda*. Hence she was jealous of her sister's progeny. She then requested and received a divine blessing that her *garuda* would have the power to eat *nagas*.

With the head, wings and lower body of an eagle and the torso and arms of a powerful man, the *garuda* is an imposing figure, as befits its exalted position. Venerated as the mount of the god Vishnu in Indian mythology, this exalted creature is accepted also in Thai tradition and serves as the insignia of the King and the Royal Kingdom. Thus besides being depicted on temples throughout the country, frequently as a central motif on decorated gables, the *garuda* is featured on the royal flag, on banknotes, on the letterhead of official documents and on the façades of businesses that have received a royal appointment from His Majesty.

There is only one *garuda* but a thousand *nagas*, divine serpents sometimes shown with multiple heads which inhabit the subterranean regions. Like its half brother, the *naga* looms large in Buddhist and Brahman cosmology and has various roles and meanings. It is the carrier of the world and descends into slumber to create a new world at the bottom of the cosmic ocean. The mythical snake is further regarded as a water symbol, as well as a representation of the rainbow in which form it serves as a bridge linking the world of man with the realm of the gods.

Specifically in Buddhist tales, the *nagas* form part of the retinue of the God of the West and a legend holds that one of the breed, named *Mucalinda*, protected the Buddha. As the story has it, the

Buddha was meditating in the sixth week after his Enlightenment, sitting exposed to the weather. Seeing this the *naga* approached and sheltered the Buddha with its coils and its hooded head.

Reminders of the event are readily witnessed today in images showing the Buddha seated on a *naga*. But as with the *garuda*, mythical snakes are portrayed in numerous ways, perhaps most commonly as balustrades flanking the steps leading to a temple – a further testament to the creature's link between earth and the heavens. In other art and decorative motifs the snakes are usually shown in the grip of the *garuda*, a reference to the lasting hostility between the two beasts.

Initially, with its great size and strength, the *garuda* could easily catch *nagas*, and even though they tried to hide beneath the water, the bird used its mighty wings to beat back the waves. Later, however, the *nagas* realized that the *garuda* could only just lift their weight and if they were slightly heavier they could ward off its attack. Thus they carried rocks in their mouths, forcing the bird to drop them before it was crushed by the returning waves.

The ploy worked for a while but was eventually defeated when the *garuda* changed its method of attack, grabbing not the head but the snakes' body and tail. In this way the dangling serpents were forced to drop the stones. This is why today the *garuda* is typically shown gripping the *naga's* body, letting its head hang down.

Yet a further account of the relations between the *nagas* and the *garuda* relates how the latter eventually achieved its exalted position among the gods. The *nagas*, wishing to become immortal, persuaded the *garuda* to steal the food of the gods for them. This the giant bird did but refrained from eating any of the ambrosia itself. Vishnu saw the *garuda's* self-control and in his praise offered to bestow a blessing. The *garuda* asked to be made immortal and when the wish was granted, it promised in return always to be Vishnu's carrier.

Monstrous though the *nagas* and the *garuda* may appear at times, they are in fact revered creatures; the part of true monster in Thai legend belongs to the *yakshas*. These are a race of giant-size demons invariably shown with cruel faces and long protruding canine teeth attesting to a notorious cannibal habit. They are supernatural beasts though not entirely separate from the human world as they can inter-marry; abducting young girls is something of a favoured pastime.

In essence *yakshas* are the bogie men of children's nightmares, although they have mixed and varied roles in their numerous appear-ances in Thai legends and classical literature. Many of the demons are specific beings with proper names and by no means are all evil or irresponsible creatures. For example, Kuvera is supreme among *yakshas*, the keeper of the North World who is entrusted with the task of examining man's actions which he accounts as sin or merit on the eight and fifteenth days of the waning and waxing moon.

Besides cropping up in myths and classic sagas like the *Ramakien*, *yakshas* are commonly encountered in the round as statuary in temple compounds where they serve as guardians. Typically they are placed in pairs flanking the compound's entrance with their backs to the temple and clutching huge clubs. Standing like sentries, their duty is to guard against any approaching devils.

Especially fine examples of *yaksha* statuary are to be seen at Bangkok's Temple of the Dawn and Temple of the Emerald Buddha. At the latter there are 12 statues which atypically face the shrine (so as to protect the image of the Emerald Buddha rather than the temple itself) and are furthered distinguished as named protagonists in the *Ramakien* epic, each being identified by a different colour. For instance, the two at the first east gate represent the red-faced Suriyaphob and the green-faced Indrachit, son of the Ramakien's demon king, Thosagan. Among the others, the two on the compound's south side, the green-bodied Thoskiriwan and the red Thoskirithorn, are set apart by having trunks instead of noses, their being Thosagan's sons born to a female elephant.

The guardian role of *yakshas* is not limited to temples – Kuvera has traditionally been accredited with the power to protect newborn children. A shaman would be called upon to draw a picture of Kuvera surrounded by magic symbols on a piece of cloth which was then suspended over a baby's cradle to ward off harmful influences. It was essential to depict Kuvera armed with his club as it was believed to be an especially potent, even magical weapon. Legend has it that Kuvera, in a former life as a human being, once threw his club like a boomerang and succeeded in crushing a thousand *yakshas* with a single swing.

If *yakshas* can be seen as the Mr Universe among Thailand's mythical population, the title of Miss Photogenic would go to the *kinnari*, a lovely creature half woman and half bird. (A less frequently depicted male counterpart is known as *kinnara*.) As with the guardian giants, *kinnaris* are popular features of temple statuary, those at the Wat Phra Keo attracting so much tourist attention that they must rank as the most photographed of Bangkok's exotic images.

Cosmic dwellers, the *kinnaris* possess the head, torso and arms of a women combined with a swan-like lower body, along with a bird's legs and tail. The anatomical mix may sound odd and cumbersome but Thai artists have imparted an essential grace and beauty to the painted and sculpted form which appears widely in classical art. In legend, these charming creatures match attractive physical attributes with accomplishments in singing and music.

As with most of Thailand's mythical beings, *kinnaris* have been adopted from neighbouring cultures, most emphatically India, but the adoption was accompanied by adaptation in terms of artistic representation. They thus look quintessentially Thai whether seen in mural paintings or gracing temple compounds.

Equally, *kinnaris* are encountered in both cosmic myths, where they serve as attendants to Kuvera, and in more strictly Buddhist legends. The best loved of the many *kinnari* incarnations is that of Princess Manohara, who appears in one of the non-canonical stories of the Buddha's previous lives. This typically convoluted fairytale romance shows the *kinnari* displaying the virtues of love, fortitude and perseverance.

Matching the *kinnari* in beauty are the *apsaras*, celestial nymphs who rose from the Sea of Milk as it was churned by the gods to take the elixir of life. Inhabiting the air above the mythical Himalayan forests, their destiny is to dance and fulfil the desires of the divinities residing on the cosmic Mount Meru. More commonly depicted in Khmer rather than Thai art, *apsaras* do make an appearance in Thailand, pictured gliding gracefully in the skies of temple mural paintings.

Other fabulous beings in the roll call of Thailand's mythical menagerie which make frequent appearance in murals and other forms of classical art include various birds and hybrid manifestations of the lion.

Ranking high among the feathered creatures is the *hong* or *hongsa*, a mythical swan. The bird is credited with superb grace and in Thai is a proverbial example of graceful beauty. In legend it is the mount of the god Brahma, the creator of the universe, and its flight is regarded as an important link between the aquatic world and the heavens above. The *hong* is thus an auspicious figure, frequently seen as the portent of a miracle.

The *hongsa* can be found in statuary and paintings, although its most famous representation is on His Majesty the King's royal barge, *Suphanahong*, the prow of which is fashioned in a stylized form of the mythical swan.

Gracing the air of the mythical Himalayan forests are other birds including the *tantima*, which stands erect and has a body similar to that of the *garuda* and a long mouth shaped like a walking stick. The *wayubhak* is a rather ordinary looking bird, though distinguished as the symbol of Thailand's financial affairs, first so used by King Narai's minister, Constantine Phaulkon, in the 17th century. More curious in appearance is the little *arahan* bird which has a human face and torso, male or female, and a bird's wings, tail and feet.

The lion, or *rajashingha*, has four major manifestations in classical depictions: *Trinnasingha* who has wings, the black *Kalasingha*,

Pandarasingha with a magnificent golden mane, and the white *Kraisornsingha* who is reputed to have a growl which can be heard throughout the animal kingdom. The latter is feared and respected while the former three are less fierce herbivores.

All these weird and wonderful beings, and others too numerous to mention, inhabited the Buddhist cosmology as presented in the *Trai Bhum* or the Three Worlds (Heaven, Earth and Hell). They also have roles to play in the major texts of classical literature, the *Ramakien* and the *Jataka* tales. These have traditionally provided the prime sources of artistic inspiration. And so observant visitors, as they admire the adornment of Thailand's temples and other stores of classical art, as well as many mundane motifs, will find themselves exploring a truly fabulous menagerie.

FOREIGNERS THROUGH THE LOOKING GLASS

Travel is possessed of an exquisite irony. Wide-eyed visitors, strangers in a strange land, gape and gawp at what is to them exotic. Rarely do they reflect that they, too, are exotic in the eyes of their hosts. While they point their cameras at the quaint street vendor, the classical dancer, or children at play, their images are being recorded in the mind's eye of their subjects.

In Thailand, long before the invention of the camera, that irony found ingenuous expression in the nation's pictorial art. Unwittingly foreigners provided painters with such a rich store of exotic motifs that when today's tourist snaps a mural painting he may well step through the looking glass and inadvertently photograph himself. Well, perhaps not quite as he looks now but certainly as his ancestors looked to the Thais of old. The image is not always flattering.

No matter how far artists internalize their vision, their ideas are always a response to external stimuli. Thus any graphic art, quite aside from all aesthetic considerations, provides to a lesser or greater degree documentation of the age and society in which it is produced. Regardless of theme and principal subject matter, a painting affords telling insights into the life and times of its historical moment.

The religious themes popular with Renaissance painters, for example, say almost as much about the landscape and architecture of 15th- and 16th-century Italy as they do about the nature of Christian faith. Similarly, the portraiture of the Dutch and Flemish masters are timeless as works of art but are rooted in the 17th century as revelations of the stolid virtues of the burgher and mercantile classes of the place and period. The painting of Thailand is no exception in its documentary value. While vastly different from that of the West in form, content and purpose, it nonetheless offers parallel images of social comment.

Temple murals, the most original and accomplished of all traditional Thai art forms, along with the skilled decorative art of gilt-on-lacquer, frequently display exotic details and cameo scenes. These are usually, though not always, extraneous to a picture's main subject and it is here that the artist found scope for exotic motifs. Not least among these are images of foreigners given fascinating and, at times, mischievous expression.

This phenomenon is especially striking since classical Thai art, in theory at least, is largely devoid not only of any tradition of realism but also of any individual self-expression. The choice of subject matter was rigidly limited. However, first impressions can be deceptive and a closer examination of murals reveals a surprising variety of incidental images.

While trained solely through copying and always working to an accepted pattern, painters were possessed of a sharp eye and were certainly not oblivious to changes in their real-life environment. At the time when painting was achieving its finest expression foreigners, in the form of mercenaries, traders, adventurers and diplomatic envoys, were increasingly visible figures in the Siamese landscape. Murals and lacquered cabinets became a mirror of the shifting scene.

Line drawing if not painting can be traced back to the first Siamese kingdom, Sukhothai, founded in the 13th century; graphic art was likely an early accomplishment of Thai civilization. From tentative beginnings mural painting reached full development in 17th-century Ayutthaya, the capital from 1350 to 1767. The art form continued to flourish in the early Bangkok period (dating from 1782 onwards), though by the first years of the 20th century it had fallen into decline, becoming repetitive and stereotyped in its inability to find new modes of expression.

Murals, complemented by pictorial adornment on doors and window shutters, were executed on each of the four interior walls of the main buildings in a temple complex, typically the *bot*, or ordination hall, and the *viharn*, the principal hall for sermons and daily use.

The primary purpose of such painting was didactic, not aesthetic nor decorative. It aimed to teach the people about the religion and to reinforce their faith in and devotion to the teachings of the Buddha. Themes and even particular scenes were standardized and the artists, often possessed of individual genius, were expected to sublimate personal expression and execute established forms with orthodox content.

Despite, or perhaps because of the severe restrictions imposed on artists in terms of subject matter, painters did seek a degree of freedom in the execution of details. It was a convention of both murals and gilt-on-lacquer decoration that the entire surface be covered with designs. Accordingly, artists found a certain scope for self-expression in backgrounds and minor details. Here are depicted superb genre scenes of daily Thai life and, almost inescapably, novel material in the strange image of the foreigner. All were shown with an uncanny realism that remarkably managed to coexist with spiritual content and didactic purpose.

At its finest this subordinated element of realism shows acute powers of observation and a marked – at times, wicked – sense of humour. The former attribute is most wonderfully seen in the portrayal of birds and animals which provides a superb natural history record. Yet it is equally apparent in scenes of contemporary life in which the foreigner was an irresistible exotic addition. Dress, racial types and facial expressions are all captured with an eye for detail.

Humour is apparent in glorious cameos of impious gaiety – a lovers' tiff, the antics of a drunkard, dogs stealing food from the cook, and so on. Not unnaturally, the foreigner with his strange ways and manners could be a figure of fun as well as an outlandish motif.

The significance of these alien images, however, transcends mere curiosity. They offer an intriguing documentation of how foreigners were perceived at various periods in Thai history. Their career in the country was a chequered one, and depending on the prevailing political climate, the tone of their portrayal ranges from the curious through the contemptuous and the comic before finally reaching something close to begrudging respect, or at least recognition as human.

The first Westerners on the scene were the Portuguese who arrived in 1511. Their colonial influence was slight and they had little time to make either negative or positive impressions on the Thais. Individuals did linger on in the country, most finding employment as mercenaries. Their pictorial representation in murals, such as it is, was thus fairly neutral and in Thonburi's Wat Suwannaram, for example, some Portuguese in rather dashing red and green uniforms are shown as pretty effectual fellows, thrusting forward with muskets.

Coinciding with the flowering of mural and gilt lacquer art was the first extensive wave of foreign arrivals which broke on the shores of Siam in the early-17th century. The Dutch came in 1604, the British in 1612 and the French in 1622. Various Europeans established themselves as traders – not always respectable – at Ayutthaya which, during the 17th-century height of its power, had a genuine cosmopolitan air. These Westerners joined various Asian foreigners -- Indians, Persians, Chinese, Japanese, Burmese – who were also engaged in the brief burst of international dealings that erupted during the reign of King Narai (1656-88).

Of all the foreigners it was the French who made the greatest impression. Their influence was short-lived – their mission being unceremoniously expelled after the Revolution of 1688 – but their two embassies from the court of King Louis XIV were much heralded and brought a colourful presence to the Siamese capital.

After the failure of the French embassies, foreigners were treated as suspect until at least the middle of the 19th century. But the impact they failed to achieve in physical presence was, albeit dubiously, maintained in the pictorial image.

Throughout the latter part of the Ayutthaya period and well into the early Bangkok era the alien images found in mural paintings alternated between the neutrally exotic and the downright derogatory.

In the first category the foreigner is employed in a picture to add 'colour', similar to the way in which tourists like to include figures that are different in their snapshots. In such poses the foreigner is depicted with fine observation for physical characteristics, clothes and typical trappings, notably horse and cannon in the case of Europeans.

The kindest illustrations of this are found on gilt and lacquer cabinets where the alien motif was frequently the main subject and covered most of the picture area. The French especially, with their elaborate frock coats, wigs and flamboyant hats, gave artists plenty of material to work with. However, Westerners were not necessarily singled out and one especially fine lacquer cabinet, now in Bangkok's National Museum, has full-length illustrations of a European and an Arab, giving it the popular name of 'Suleiman and Louis XIV' (not that the figures necessarily represent those historical personages).

In mural painting the artists were less generous. They did employ alien images simply for exotic effect and in Wat Ko Kaeo Suttharam in Petchburi there is a figure of mostly probably a Jesuit dressed as a Buddhist monk. It is a mere curiosity.

In the same temple, however, the murals, dated 1734, also depict a whole register of foreigners posed as divinities flying through the air mostly in gestures of adoration. It is a classic mural scene of *Vidhyadharas* (literally celestial beings that have attained wisdom), except each figure is different and given the very recognizable facial characteristics of variously the Indians, Chinese, French, Khmer, Japanese, Burmese and others. The series is largely a neutral portrayal yet many of the faces border on the comical if not quite the grotesque. It is worth noting that Thai mythology accounts for not only benevolent but also malicious *Vidhyadharas*.

Such figures may be borderline cases between the exotic and the derogatory, though another classic mural scene, 'The Victory Over Mara', leaves no doubt as to how some artists viewed the foreigner. Of all the conventional mural subjects, Mara gave painters the greatest scope for invention and self expression. In it are massed all the forces of evil, a convoluted heap of warring elements, humans, monsters, devils and demons. Displaying admirable panache – one can almost imagine the artists chuckling to themselves as they worked – painters went to town on this scene and the foreigner was an irresistible addition to the composition, a fresh image to boost the ranks of evil. The Frenchman, with coat tails flapping as he rides blithely into the fray, was a popular figure, while other aliens are drawn with expressions ranging from the villainous to the vacuous.

Since Siam was virtually closed to the outside world during the 18th century, it was not until the mid-19th century that the pictorial representation of the foreigner ceased to swing between the decoratively neutral and the amusingly derogatory. In the 1850s King Mongkut began normalizing foreign relations and opened up the country to international trade. From this time on the image of the foreigner becomes more individual and more human in context. Sailors and merchants, for example, are seen quite naturally for what they are.

Now begins a new chapter in Thai painting and positive foreign influences were not limited to trade. King Mongkut's interest in things Western went beyond commerce and extended into the realm of ideas and aesthetics. During his reign and that of his successors European art styles and conventions were incorporated to varying degrees in the work of mural painters.

The most celebrated artist of the period, and indeed the most revolutionary of all mural painters, was Khrua In Khong. Although working within the convention of the religious mural, he deviated from tradition in both style and inspiration. For the latter he drew less on the life of the Buddha and more on allegorical scenes expressing Buddhist ideas. Some of the best and most striking of these unusual paintings adorn the walls of Wat Bovorniwet in Bangkok.

Stylistic changes, however, were even more striking. Influenced by the prevailing interest in things Western, Khrua In Khong was the first Thai painter to attempt three-dimensional perspective and to use a wider range of colours, especially sombre tones, to create mood. He also chose to illustrate his allegories with scenes of Western architecture and landscapes peopled with European figures. The dress of the latter and details of the former are all minutely observed. So too are material phenomena of the times, such as sailing ships and horse races.

With the work of Khrua In Khong the Western pictorial image in Thai art first comes of age. No longer either a naïve exotic motif or a disparaging image, the alien is genuinely explored in the artist's dual concern with giving Buddhist allegory fresh expression and with studying the historical moment.

Khrua In Khong, much admired by King Mongkut, was popular and influential in his day, yet despite a number of followers, his achievement stands on its own. Instead of having the effect of injecting fresh life into mural painting, his work survives as a glorious burst of one man's genius just before the art form went into sharp decline.

Luckily for the Westerner's amour propre, mural painting did treat him with something approaching respect before it finally ran out of ideas. In a graphic turn-of-the-century record, the murals of the Song Panuat building at Wat Benchamabopit display scenes from the life of King Chulalongkorn in which Westerners, soldiers and even individuals such as the Austrian ambassador are depicted as positive historical images. As Thailand began to consolidate its place on the world stage, so did its art reflect a normalization of international relations.

One scene in the 'Song Panuat' series begs special mention for its prophetic content. A man accompanied by his wife and decked out in tropical suit and solar topee is pictured gawping at a performance of street theatre. He is for all the world a tourist. Perhaps life does mirror art after all.

THE 'RAMAKIEN' IN THAI ARTS

It sounds a heady brew. 'A work combining the popularity of the Arthurian legends, the literary force of the works of Shakespeare and the authority of the Bible.'

Thus one art historian sums up the *Ramakien*, the epic tale that has shaped classical Thai arts more than any other secular influence. It provides story lines for dance drama, puppet plays and shadow theatre, while its huge cast of gorgeously attired heroes and hideously masked demons people the pictorial world of murals, bas reliefs, sculpture and the decorative arts.

Such is the all-pervading influence of the *Ramakien* that nothing would appear more Thai. Ironically it is not strictly a home-grown product but rather the local version of the Indian *Ramayana* epic, and its roll call of gods and demons belongs essentially to the Hindu world of the Subcontinent rather than to the Theravada Buddhist land of the Thais. Most cultures of South-East Asia, however, are rooted in Indian influences which gradually infiltrated the region from around the 2nd century AD onwards.

Religious, mythological, linguistic and other elements of Indian culture were implanted by absorption rather than conquest and colonization, and thus became especially persuasive. The various local populations adapted and moulded Indian influences to their own ways, gradually evolving cultures that were distinct yet with common roots.

Among the cultural imports were the Sanskrit classics whose themes were eventually to provide a narrative source for the visual and performing arts in Thailand. Most influential of all was the *Ramayana* which, along with the *Mahabarat*, ranks as India's greatest literary work.

Written some 2,000 years ago and accredited to the Indian poet Valmiki, the *Ramayana* opens with the founding of the rival cities of Ayutthaya, capital of the gods, and Langka, city of the demons. The long and convoluted tale revolves around the struggle between these two antagonistic forces, the principal action focusing on the trials and tribulations of Ayutthaya's Prince Rama, the abduction of his wife, Sita, and the eventual defeat of Langka by Hanuman and his army of monkey warriors.

Like all the best stories, the *Ramayana* combines adventure and excitement – plus a touch of comic relief – with moral edification. At the same time, full play is given to strange occurrences in which magic, divination, horoscopes and other mysteries are important elements.

The epic, in one form or another, was incorporated in the cultures of almost all South-East Asian civilizations and was firmly established before the rise of the Thai kingdom. But while the *Ramayana's* influence stretches way back, the Thai version, the *Ramakien*, is a distinctly local creation, as exemplified by the text of King Rama I, composed in 1807.

It is not known how far Rama I relied on the vernacular versions of the story that had been passed down through the centuries, nor to what extent he consulted Indian sources, yet it is important to note that he did not merely translate the *Ramayana*. His *Ramakien* is a characteristically Thai version, adapted to the Thai world.

The narrative follows the Indian story only in its broad outlines and there are considerable differences in detail. Names are modified and dress, customs, ways of life, even the flora assume local distinction. As art historian Jean Boisselier has written: 'Based on an Indian plot, gradually modified in South-East Asia – as is proved by 12th century evidence at Angkor Wat – the chronicle of Rama finally acquired in Thailand a character that may properly be described as Thai.'

A classic though it is, the *Ramakien*, unlike the literary land-marks of the West, has impact not through the pages of a handsomely bound book but via myriad art forms. The incomparably rich text, again in the words of Boisselier, 'lends itself naturally to illustration, whether painterly or graphically, or to theatre in all its forms.'

One the most accessible manifestations of the *Ramakien's* visual impact is encountered at Wat Po (Temple of the Reclining Buddha) Bangkok's oldest and largest temple complex. Here, on the outer wall of the main chapel, is a series of marble bas reliefs depicting a selection of connected scenes from the epic tale in a set of 152 panels, each some 45 centimetres (18 inches) square.

The theme of the reliefs is drawn from the middle section of the *Ramakien* and portrays the abduction and subsequent rescue of Sita. For some strange reason, the panels conclude not with the stirring climax of the victory over Langka but with the death of a minor character before the defeat of Thotsakan and the recovery of Sita. This is perhaps because the artists simply ran out of space – and the lack of a proper conclusion would not have been deemed unsatisfactory by an audience familiar with the tale since childhood. Moreover, such is the artistic skill that each panel can be regarded as a minor work of art in itself.

Wat Po also illustrates the power of the *Ramakien* in a different medium. This is found in the exquisite mother-of-pearl inlay work that decorates the doors of the main chapel with scenes from the epic. Mother-of-pearl inlay art, in which cut pieces are glued on to a paper cartoon, then applied to a permanent and subsequently lacquered surface, has a long tradition in Thailand. It reached its zenith in the mid-19th century, though the doors at Wat Po present exceptionally fine examples.

In painting, the influence of the *Ramakien* on temple murals can be seen at nearby Wat Phra Keo (Temple of the Emerald Buddha), in the grounds of the Grand Palace. Here, scenes comprising a complete series of illustrations from the *Ramakien*, inspired by the text of Rama I, cover the walls of the temple cloisters. The original painting dates from the early 19th century but although some of the compositions are remarkable, the work as a whole has suffered from repeated and poorly executed attempts at restoration. The worst damage resulted from a complete re-painting in 1932, when Bangkok was spruced up in preparation for its 150th anniversary.

By this time the art of traditional mural painting was in decline and the artists entrusted with the restoration, while respecting the original compositions, introduced Western notions of volume, shadow and graduated colour. This radically altered the character of the scenes and debased their aesthetic value. Nonetheless the Wat Phra Keo murals remain a good example of the *Ramakien's* pictorial influence, if not of Thai classical painting's true achievement.

Another medium of the visual arts to draw on the pictorial potential of the *Ramakien* is gilt-on-lacquer. Employed to decorate numerous objects from small boxes to entire wooden panels, it is perhaps most effectively displayed on Thai manuscript cabinets. The art form, which comprises designs in gold leaf on a generally black background, was introduced from China during the Ayutthaya period and peaked from the 17th to the mid-18th century. After the fall of Ayutthaya in 1767, however, the art of transposing the subjects of wall paintings into lacquer was developed. Accordingly new heights of achievement were attained during the Ratanakosin, or Bangkok, era – as demonstrated by the cabinets of the Buddhaisawan Chapel in the compound of Bangkok's National Museum.

With reference to this, Jean Boisselier has remarked: 'Since lacquers now exploited technical possibilities to the full, they displayed truly monumental proportions on relatively small surfaces. In this connection – especially in the scenes from the *Ramakien* – the cabinets preserved in Buddhaisawan Chapel represent one of the peaks not only of the art of lacquer and of classical Thai painting, but of a genre which can legitimately be classed among the choicest examples of world painting.'

Predating the *Ramakien's* influence on the visual arts was its popularity with the various forms of traditional theatre. Earliest of the performing arts was the *nang* shadow plays. The name literally means 'hide' or 'skin', and the performance is by cut-out buffalo-hide figures held aloft on two sticks and presented as transparencies against an illuminated screen. This type of theatre probably originated in India and eventually found its way to Thailand via Java. It is not known exactly when it was adopted by the Thais; its first recorded mention is in the Palatine Law proclaimed by King Borom Trailokanath of Ayutthaya in 1458.

The *nang yai* (literally 'large hide') form of the play takes its story direct from the *Ramakien* and several hundred cut-out figures depict single and paired characters against intricate backgrounds of palaces, landscapes and other scenes. A full performance would take some 720 hours to stage, commonly a selection of episodes, or 'sets', of proven popularity constituted a single show.

Today, *nang yai* is a dying art and performances are rarely staged. Nonetheless, examples of the cut-out figures, some dating from the reign of King Rama II (1809-24), can be seen at the National Museum in Bangkok. These exhibits, in the absence of living shadow theatre, attest to the dominant influence of the *Ramakien* on one of Thailand's most formative theatre arts.

Directly related to shadow plays, and fortunately in a less moribund state, is the *khon* masked dance drama which again takes its narrative content from the *Ramakien*. A former court entertainment and probably the best known style of Thai classical dance, *khon* dates from the 16th century and was originally performed exclusively by male actors, all of whom wore ornate masks. Today, conventions have been relaxed, although the demon and monkey characters are still masked. Attired in rich costumes, the actors communicate by complex and stylized hand gestures and body movements, which express both action and emotions. This mute performance is accompanied by an orchestra and a chorus.

Like shadow theatre, *khon* usually consists of various episodes from the *Ramakien*. Set pieces, with emotive titles such as 'The Conquest of the Demon Crow' or 'The Fire – The Ordeal of Sita', have always been favoured over any possible abridgment of the lengthy saga. So familiar were audiences with the tale that selections could be appreciated as complete performances and programmes could be varied according to popular demand.

A traditional performing art akin to *khon* and shadow plays is *hun* puppet theatre. Featuring minutely detailed marionettes representing characters from the *Ramakien*, *hun* puppets were operated by strings from below and skilfully manipulated to imitate with amazing faithfulness the actions of *khon* dancers.

Sadly, as with many other types of traditional arts, *hun* puppet shows are now all but extinct. The passing of such wonderful entertainments is to be regretted but the inspiration behind them lives on. There can be little doubt that the chronicle of Rama, with all its adventures, magic and deeper meanings impinging on so many aspects of Thai culture, will remain immortal.

THAI CLASSICAL DANCE DRAMA

She moves with mesmerizing grace. Gorgeously adorned with tapering gilded crown and silver-embroidered costume, she slowly twists and turns, lifting a foot and effortlessly raising and lowering the body all the while tracing a beguiling pattern with outstretched hands and backward-curving fingers.

To say that the Thais have innate grace is a travel brochure cliché, yet watching a classical dancer perform is to glimpse a certain truth behind the stereotype. Although the traditional performing arts are not as vibrant as they once were, suffering inroads by Western entertainments and generally changing tastes, Thai dance drama is not extinct. What survives displays the elegance of an art form refined over centuries and supported by regal patronage.

The Thais reputedly first acquired a dance troupe when, in AD 1431, they conquered the ancient Khmer capital of Angkor and took as part of their booty an entire corps de ballet, dancers whose performances had once been seen as a symbolic link between earth and the realm of the gods. Cultural transfer through conquest was then common in South-East Asia, although the Thais always adapted whatever they acquired, thus over time they developed various forms of dance in a style inimitably their own. The typically elaborate masks and costumes, for example, owe more to Thai innovation than to ancient Khmer traditions.

Leaving aside folk and regional dances (southern Thailand's

Indian-influenced *manohra* dance, for example), the two major forms of Thai classical dance drama are *khon* and *lakon nai*. In the beginning both were exclusively court entertainments, it was not until much later that a popular style of dance theatre, *likay*, evolved as a diversion for the common folk who had no access to royal performances.

All three forms still survive as live theatre, but only just. Most commonly visitors will glimpse classical dancers at Bangkok's Erawan Shrine, where they perform as a votive offering for supplicants, or catch snippets of traditional dance dramas featured in the cultural shows put on by various Bangkok restaurants. Yet neither display offers a full appreciation of an art form whose repertoire was once sufficient to sustain performances lasting an entire day. Fortunately, however, the Fine Arts Department's Division of Music and Dance strives to preserve the classical forms with integrity, training both performers and teachers to a high standard of proficiency. Providing a showcase for these efforts is Bangkok's National Theatre, home of the country's only professional classical dance troupe, which stages regular performances of both *khon* and *lakon nai*, generally in a mixed three-hour programme.

As a base art form, *likay* lacks an equivalent champion although, despite being challenged by travelling film shows in rural areas, it clings to a degree of popularity in the provinces and still has the power to draw attentive audiences at temple fairs and other festive occasions. Essentially, *likay* is a bastardized manifestation of dance drama, drawing on various sources and pandering to popular taste, frequently involving somewhat earthy, if not downright crude, humour.

In contrast, *khon* and *lakon nai* are strictly classical and highly stylized. Each is a distinct form of dance drama, although there are shared aspects which distinguish Thai theatre in general.

Most famous of the two is *khon* which is a masked dance dramatization of the *Ramakien*, described in the previous chapter. Developing out of shadow-play in the 16th century, a full *khon* performance demands a vast cast of actors playing the roles of gods, giants, men, monkey warriors and assorted beasts. All the characters were at one time depicted by the actors wearing elaborate masks but in latter-day shows only the masks of giants and animals have been retained. Nevertheless, any narrative is still left to a chorus and actors keep their faces expressionless, communicating solely through a complex vocabulary of hand gestures and body movements.

Whereas *khon* portrays exclusively the *Ramakien* story, *lakon nai* may take its narrative content from a variety of legends, the *Inaw*, another princely tale, being one of the most popular. A further difference is that masks are not worn by *lakon nai* dancers.

Traditionally *lakon nai* was danced exclusively by women and the *khon* only by men. Such a division between the sexes is no longer strictly adhered to but it does point to a more vital distinction between the two dramatic styles. While both forms rely on gesture and posture as modes of expressing emotion as well as action, there is a fundamental difference in emphasis. Whereas the *khon* actor seeks virtuosity in strength and agility and muscular exertion, the *lakon nai* dancer is persuasive through grace and remarkably controlled movement. Each traces intricate patterns of motion, through hand, arm and the studied raising and lowering of the body, yet the male's movements are emphatic and staccato in execution while the female's are more fluid and subtly beguiling.

Serving as a counterpoint to the control and restraint of the dance itself are the costumes which, even aside from the superb masks used in *khon*, are extremely rich and flamboyant. Made of intricately embroidered cloth, the attire of a leading male comprises a tight-fitting jacket, breeches and a loin cloth worn outside and held in place by a broad sash and a bejewelled belt. Ornaments such as bracelets, armlets and rings add further to a picture of sartorial splendour. For female players the typical dress is a long skirt and cape – though such prosaic terms scarcely do justice to the gorgeous way in which the costumes are fashioned – pointed golden headdress and other jewellery that rivals if not surpasses the glory of the male.

Dancers do not wear make-up as in the Western theatrical tradition, where it is used to alter appearance to a greater or lesser extent. Instead, facial features are merely accentuated in the usual manner. The *khon* masks are similarly conventional in the way that they depend on colour symbolism and stylized design to depict the various characters, rather than make any attempt to portray the life-like. Each mask, however, is distinctive and all are splendid examples of traditional Thai decorative art.

Music is integral to all forms of Thai dance drama and *khon* and *lakon nai* performances are accompanied by an orchestra comprising traditional instruments – usually five percussion pieces and one woodwind. Small bell-like cymbals are used to set the pace while the music of the rest of the orchestra lends mood. Like most other aspects of classical Thai theatre, the orchestra is bound by convention. Essentially the tunes are indicative of specific actions and emotions, so there are 'walking tunes', 'marching tunes', 'laughing tunes', 'weeping tunes', 'anger tunes' and so on. Such musical passages are instantly recognizable by an audience accustomed to Thai musical notation and composition.

Familiarity is, indeed, a key to appreciation not only of the music but also of the entire performance. Unlike Western drama, classical Thai dramatic art is static in content. Audiences never demanded fresh stories, delighting instead in the presentation of well-loved tales so familiar that favourite episodes could be enjoyed out of context from their larger narrative.

Conservatism and stylization are quintessential; everything is precise and restrained according to custom. Nothing is spontaneous. Performances are mostly slow and formal, although a certain liveliness is found in set comic interludes and battle scenes. As a spectacle, the dance mesmerizes by its grace and dignity, and by a sense of the fabulous emphasized by the performers' masks and costumes.

None of it comes easy; years of training lie behind a dancer's performance. As with ballet lessons for Western children, classical Thai dance is taught to enthusiastic youngsters from a tender age, while formal training at the College of Dramatic Art in Bangkok involves a six-year high-school programme, after which the best students will go on to complete a four-year bachelor's degree course. Although study is tougher than at ordinary schools, involving physical as well as mental training, classical dance courses remain surprisingly popular and currently there are some 8,000 students enrolled at the College of Dramatic Art and its 11 sister schools in the provinces.

Pupils study both the usual academic subjects as well as dance, for which there are different training programmes depending on the style of dance and the student's own suitability. For the young *khon* dancer, for example, roles are divided into four categories: male human, female human (usually played by male dancers), demonic and simian. Each has its own style of movement and before training begins students are selected according to which parts they are best suited to. A short, stocky lad is perfect for a simian role, while a big fellow with long limbs is ideal to play an ogre.

The budding *lakon nai* performer, on the other hand, must memorize the *mae bot*, the 'mother alphabet of dance' which contains 64 basic gestures and patterns of movement, before learning how to combine these in interpretive dancing. After basic specialization, training for both *khon* and *lakon nai* players involves increasing sophistication and perfection, along with more complex theory and tuition in choreography and stage management.

If *khon* and *lakon nai* can be compared as art to Western ballet, *likay* is the equivalent of pantomime. King Rama VI, a monarch noted for his knowledge of the theatre, wrote it was 'popular with a certain class of people who are not very discriminating in their taste.' The saving grace of *likay*, however, is that it has no pretensions to being other than entertainment.

In form, *likay* basically parodies *lakon nai* (though its origins also owe something to Chinese opera), and the dramatic content is standard, full of the tried and tested stuff of melodrama – crossed lovers, maidens in distress, lost princes finally reunited with their patrimony, and so forth. Improvization plays an important part and one performance can differ markedly from another depending on the quickness of the actors' wit and the fertility of their sense of humour. Puns, verbal virtuosity and slap-stick humour are *likay's* stock-in-trade.

Similar to the free-flow manner of dialogue and action, costumes are allowed to run riot and there is a tendency towards gaudy jewellery, bright colours and generally raffish dress. All together, as one commentator has aptly remarked, it amounts to 'imaginative bad taste'. Make-up, too, is grossly accentuated with a liberal use of powder, rouge, lipstick and mascara.

Popular in every sense, *likay* is a sort of theatre-by-the-people-for-the-people; unlike *khon* and *lakon nai*, it is not hidebound by convention and everyone is out for a good time. And therein lies its attraction: it has, at its best, panache, verve and drive, even a strong degree of earthiness. What it lacks in artistic control its makes up for in sheer exuberance and inventive energy.

At one time no fair or country celebration was considered complete without a *likay* show and if no longer as popular as it once was, this form of theatre is essentially flexible and capable of adapting to changing tastes. Not so with *khon* and *lakon nai*, although with the continued enrolment of students at the 12 classical dance schools nationwide, there is still at least a tenuous hold on tradition.

With limited openings for professional performers, however, most graduates will eventually find themselves in the classroom as teachers rather than on the stage. But some are lucky. Backstage at the Mandarin Oriental hotel's Thai cultural show, dancer Sarin Suksomboon is ready to perform, her face flawlessly made up, her slim figure dazzlingly costumed. It's taken her just half an hour to transform herself from a modern young girl in jeans into the perfect model of a classical Thai dancer – petite, coyly pretty and graceful in every move, a fairy princess standing a fraction over one and a half metres (five foot).

Waiting patiently to go on stage, she absent-mindedly bends back the fingers of first her right hand and then the left. 'We're taught this at college to make the hands supple,' she explains. 'Every day the teacher gets us to push our fingers as far back as we can and hold the position to the count of a hundred.' After 10 years' training at Bangkok's College of Dramatic Art, it seems as if she hasn't a bone in her hand.

Being supple and able to twist the hands and body into the language of dance is not, however, what Sarin finds hardest. 'Learning to use the eyes and the smile is the most difficult.' she says. 'My favourite form of dance is *lakon nai* and to be really good you have to know how to express a whole range of emotions with the face as well as with hand and body gestures.'

Sarin began dancing at the age of 12 and now, at 22, she still has a further two year's study before completing her BA. In the mean-time she performs four nights a week at the Mandarin Oriental. She counts herself lucky to have this part-time work and has no illusions about the difficulty of surviving as a classical dancer in the modern age. 'Most dancers in Thailand, unlike overseas, work part time as the pay is very low and there is not so much work,' she says. 'The only sure way of making a career out of dancing is to become a teacher, but that's not for me and I hope eventually to get a job in television or maybe just in an office, although I'll try to continue dancing part time.'

So, if dancing is not the road to fame and fortune, what's the attraction? With a disarmingly childlike smile Sarin replies, 'Because it's beautiful. I love the costumes and rich decorations. Also it gives me pride. It's unique to Thailand, no other country has the same dance. Being a dancer, I feel I am supporting Thai culture.' The fact that dance will not support her seems of little consequence as she glides off to take her turn on stage.

THE
SPORTING WORLD

Thais are as football crazy as the rest of the world, yet the traditional sport of Muay Thai, *Thai kick boxing, remains hugely popular and even attracts Western aficionados. Kite-flying is another sport with its roots far back in Thai history and kite contests, though not as common as they once were, are still fought by dedicated groups of enthusiasts.*

MUAY THAI

As soon as the referee has given his final instructions and the seconds are out of the ring, the action is fast and furious. There is little of the face-off seen in Western fights and after a feint or two, the antagonists are at each other immediately in a flurry of lashing arms and legs, kicks to the face, elbow jabs to the back of the neck or kidneys, knee jabs into stomachs. The crowd of spectators is hardly less animated with raucous yelling of variously encouragement or abuse, and frantic gesticulations as bets are signalled across the packed arena.

Thai kick boxing, or *Muay Thai* as it correctly termed, is Thailand's unique national sport, traditionally the top spectator attraction and still managing to hold its own in the face of today's football mania. With two stadiums in Bangkok, fights are staged most nights of the week, while there is also television coverage. Outside the capital, upcountry stadiums and provincial fairs further feed the popularity of *Muay Thai*. Moreover, fighters command great respect from the public and although it is primarily a male sport, female and even transsexual boxers have won movie star-like fame.

As with Western-style boxing, fighters have gloved fists but conventional punches are employed far less and it is the use of feet, knees and elbows that does the real damage. That may make it all sound like a vicious brawl, though the reality is that *Muay Thai* is considered an art and boxers are highly skilled, totally disciplined and, not least, superbly fit.

Accounting for *Muay Thai's* popularity and the dedication of its practitioners is the sport's long and illustrious tradition that stretches far back in Thailand's history, where it has always been unbounded by any class distinction, kings and commoners having been adept in the art. Its origins lie in an ancient style of martial art dating back to at least the early 15th century, when it was used in warfare and formed an essential part of military training.

Most famously, the martial art was given prominence by King Naresuan (reigned 1590-1605) who when still a young prince was taken prisoner during one of the many battles with the Burmese during this period. Knowing of his prowess in unarmed combat, his captors gave him the chance of fighting Burma's best in one-on-one contests to win his freedom. He duly defeated all his opponents and so was able to return to Thailand a hero. From that time on *Muay Thai* began to be widely taught among the Siamese and became an essential component of a soldier's skill in warfare.

Further royal support of the martial art came in the early years of the 18th century when the aptly named King Sua, 'The Tiger King' (reigned 1703-09), had the reputation of being a ferocious *Muay Thai* fighter and such was his love of the sport that he reputedly travelled the country incognito to temple fairs and fought with anyone who would take up his challenge.

In those more violent days, *Muay Thai* was rougher and wilder than today. Strangle holds, kicks to the groin, head butting, biting, hair pulling and hip and shoulder throws were all then permitted and no gloves were worn, the hands being bandaged with hemp rope that sometimes had glued layers of ground glass for extra impact. There was no fixed ring, no three-minute rounds and the winner was the man left standing.

From the age of the 'Tiger King' until modern times, *Muay Thai* was both the sport of the people, rich and poor, and a military fighting skill but since the early decades of the 20th century it has evolved with the changing times. In the 1920s, for example, it ceased to be a part of the school curriculum and in the 1930s international boxing style rules were adopted, along with weight divisions and padded gloves. So *Muay Thai* was brought from the battlefield into the sporting arena as a cleaner though still fierce fight.

Boxing skills are taught in numerous small camps around Bangkok and in the provinces, where youngsters begin to learn the sport from the age of about 13, living in basic conditions and virtually devoting their entire time to the sport. Dedication is matched by high moral standards and in addition to teaching boxing skills, trainers instil in their students the importance of good conduct and manners, and patience.

Like much else in Thai culture, ritual surrounds *Muay Thai* and how a bout is conducted, its context as it were, adds considerably to the fascination of the contest. Setting the atmosphere is the musical accompaniment of staccato drum beats and the high-pitched wavering tones of Thai flutes, the sounds variously eerie or stirring according to the tempo which rises and falls in accordance with the action.

Further adding to the sport's uniqueness are the elaborate preliminaries before a bout. After entering the ring, each boxer pays respects to his teacher, kneeling and facing the direction of his training camp, home or birthplace. He raises his gloved fists to his forehead and utters a short prayer, bowing three times and lowering his gloves to touch the canvas.

The boxer then performs a *ram muay*, a varied but always complex and often balletic sequence of movements, some slow-motion boxing moves, others less obvious flowing or rocking actions. This display may last for up to five minutes or so and is enthusiastically appreciated by the crowd. Ostensibly the *ram muay* is designed to steady the nerves and serve as a warm-up exercise, though there are more arcane motives, as when a boxer walks around the ring sliding one glove along the top rope to ensure evil spirits are kept away, or literally stamping the presence of his aura in each of the four corners of the ring. Even hexing, usually by drawing a line with the toe, is another variation of the pre-fight ritual.

Not just a thrilling sporting contest between two skilled athletes, *Muay Thai* is truly Thai.

BATTLE OF THE SEXES

Every year between February and April, when the south-west monsoon prevails, a fever grips the Thais. It is contagious, affecting young and old alike and, as with so many other fevers, it is borne by the air. It is the kite and kite-flying in Thailand fires an enthusiasm that is nothing short of feverish.

During the tropical summer, peaking in the hottest month of April, the skies above open spaces in cities, towns and villages throughout the Kingdom are alive with kites wheeling and weaving in the warm air. In Bangkok, the action is focused on the Phra Mane Ground where the gilded spires and soaring roofs of the Grand Palace provide a fairy-tale backdrop to hundreds of enthusiasts, young and old, flying kites of all descriptions, picture kites of long-tailed dragons, twisting cobras, flirtatious butterflies, or familiar cartoon characters, as well as more traditional shapes.

One afternoon, a friend and long-time kite flier invited me to join him at the Phra Mane Ground. 'Just what's the attraction?' I asked as he assembled the delicate bamboo struts of a monster kite. 'Well, you can feel a bit of a fool at first,' he replied, 'a grown man standing there holding the end of a string and staring up into the sky. But once you forget yourself, you get caught up in the excitement of controlling something in an element where you cannot follow. You're on the ground, the kite's in the air but it's you that's making it all happen. Go on, go fly a kite.'

I took his advice in the way it was meant and, clutching the hand of my young daughter so that onlookers would think I was only satisfying a child's whim, I bought a rainbow-coloured cobra from one of the many vendors whose strings of kites fringe the Phra Mane Ground like rows of exotic washing lines. After a few failed runs we got the kite into the air with greater ease than I expected. It was only my daughter crying 'My go, my go' that made me realize I'd been hogging the string, completely wrapped up in what I was discovering was an enthralling pastime. In Thailand, it is also an ancient sport dignified by rules and regulations and a heritage involving kings and commoners.

Like many other forms of popular culture, the sport of kite-flying in Thailand has been handed down from generation to generation. Its origins are obscure, rooted perhaps in ancient China, although it seems probable that Thai kites are as old as the Kingdom itself. If legend is to be believed, one of the early kings of Sukhothai, the first Thai capital founded in the 13th century, was a kite enthusiast. The story has it that King Sri Indradit was one day led to the home of a beautiful noblewoman while following the string of a runaway kite and a romance blossomed.

On somewhat firmer historical ground, it is known from surviving chronicles that kites were a feature of a ceremony known as *Klang,* which was conducted by Brahman priests who then, as even now, performed royal rites. The ritual, most likely of Indian origin, involved the flying of humming *ngao* kites over the city either as a form of blessing or in order to predict the weather of the coming season.

The *Klang* ceremony survived the eclipse of Sukhothai and continued to be performed during the period when Ayutthaya was the capital (1350–1767). Kite-flying was not, however, merely a matter of ritual, it was a craze enjoyed by everyone from the king down. Such was the popularity that it is recorded that kites often became entangled with the roofs of the royal palace, not only damaging buildings but also infringing on the private preserve of the monarch. Eventually a royal edict had to be proclaimed forbidding the flying of kites over the palace; offenders were to have one hand cut off as punishment.

The Ayutthaya kings, however, were by no means anti-kite and, like their Sukhothai predecessors, were fond of the sport. In the 17th century, the French emissary to the court of King Narai, Monsieur de la Loubère, commented on how the king's kite could be seen at night with lanterns attached to it and 'glowing like a comet'. At other times a coin would be tied to the kite and if it got lost the person who recovered it could keep the money as a reward.

Other monarchs of Ayutthaya made use of kites as unlikely weapons of war. During the reign of King Phra Phetracha (1688–1703), rebels at Nakhon Ratchasima were defeated when pots of gunpowder with long fuses were attached to kites flown over the city's walls. The resulting aerial bombardment set fire to houses and caused sufficient havoc for the king's army to storm the fortifications which they had been unable to breach by conventional siege tactics.

It was also during the Ayutthaya period that the competitive kites known as *Chula* and *Pakpao* made their first appearance and competitions were organized as a national sport. An undated book titled *The Traditional Culture of Ayutthaya* records how the king would put up his *Chula* kite from the palace compound and challenge any *Pakpao* kite that entered his territory. When one did, the king would appoint royal guards to manipulate the *Chula* and bring down the intruder.

Ayutthaya eventually fell to the Burmese in 1767 but once the nation had rallied itself and Bangkok had been established as the new capital in 1782, kite-flying was once again a royal pastime. Chronicles of the period recount how King Rama II (1809–24) would fly his *Chula* kite out from his palace over the nearby residence of his brother, holding the rank of Second King, who would send up a *Pakpao* in competition.

From then on references to kites and kite-flying became much more common and the subject is featured in both history books and Thai literature. Notably, Sunthornphu, the foremost literary figure in the early Bangkok period, wrote a poetic description of how the little "female" *Pakpao* kite seduces a "male" *Chula*: '*Pakpao* has caught her *Chula* in the air... the *Chula* tilts and limps to one side barely able to balance... the *Pakpao* follows suit, she moves closer and closer. The big *Chula* struggles nearly out of control. The *Pakpao* takes aim and does not miss. Unable to move he cannot escape... finally they land and become one.'

It is not known how or when the *Chula* and *Pakpao* kites first became associated with, respectively, male and female roles. It probably has always been the case and was certainly well established by the 1800s when a French traveller, Ruth Benedict, likened the usual dominance of *Chulas* to that of males in the Thai society of the time. Thai writers in the 19th century also used the kites as male-female metaphors. 'Your beauty makes me grow fonder and fonder... But now you fly away like the *Pakpao*, moving so rapidly on the wind,' penned a royal bodyguard turned poet in the reign of King Rama III (1824–51).

On a more prosaic level, a 19th-century French traveller wrote in a letter home: 'In France kites may only be for children, but it is not so in Siam. When the strong winds come from the south you can see squadrons of big kites competing in the sky. Young men and boys will be screaming while their eyes watch passionately, for this is a serious betting game.'

Proof that kite-flying was indeed a serious and popular sport can be found in a 1921 textbook on the subject by Phraya Bhirom Bhakdi. This is the definitive work, detailing all aspects of the sport from kite-making to techniques of flying and the more aggressive skills needed for competitions. It even includes tips for gambling on kite contests.

While fun has long been enjoyed in flying any kite in Thailand, it is the *Chula/Pakpao* contests that are the true sport, what traditional Thai kite-flying is all about. Made of bamboo and paper, the *Chula* is a sturdy 2.5-metre (8½-foot) kite in the shape of a five-pointed star, equipped with three sets of bamboo barbs attached to the string and flown competitively by a team of at least 20 men and boys.

The diamond-shaped *Pakpao* is much smaller at just 89 centimetres (35 inches) and requires a team of only five fliers. Although seemingly an easy prey to the *Chula's* barbs, the kite is protected by its greater manoeuvrability, while attacking strength lies in its long tail and a loop of string hanging beneath the flying line, both of which can snare and strangle an opponent. With an expert on the string, the flighty little *Pakpao* can dart in on the more cumbersome *Chula* with deadly accuracy.

In formal competitions, needing at least two *Pakpao* teams for each *Chula* team, a field is divided across by a rope. The upwind half is *Chula* territory from where the great 'male' kites are launched across the border into the downwind half of the field where in a clear blue summer sky the 'female' *Pakpaos* flutter in swarms like so many high-flying butterflies. The object of the game is to see how many *Pakpaos* a *Chula* can bring down into its territory, or vice versa, in a 45 minute period. It might sound simple, but great skill, speed and wily tactics are displayed by masters of the sport.

The battle of the sexes between *Chula* and *Pakpao* kites was first held as an organized sport in Bangkok in 1906 at Dusit Palace. To the background music of a court orchestra and with members of his royal family in attendance, King Chulalongkorn presided over a contest in which teams competed for a royal gold cup. The event, which became known as the 'King's Cup', proved so popular that it was held annually until Chulalongkorn's death in 1910.

Without King Chulalongkorn's encouragement the contests fell into disarray until his successor, King Rama VI (1910–25) saw the need to re-establish the sport and appointed Phraya Bhirom Bhakdi to form a 'Siam Sports Club' and authorized him to hold kite-flying contests. Subsequently, World War II brought an inevitable halt to the annual *Chula* and *Pakpao* contests but since 1952 the King's Cup competition has been an annual event at the Phra Mane Ground, where in March visitors can still witness this time-honoured sport.

Alive though it remains, kite-flying has, like so many other traditional sports and pastimes, lost ground in recent years and compared to 20 teams in the 1960s, *Chula* and *Pakpao* contests these days can muster only three teams. The sport has its champion, however, in the Thai Kite Heritage Group which, since its founding in 1985, has kept *Chulas* and *Pakpaos* flying high at kite festivals in Asia, the US and Europe, as well as in Thailand. In addition, the Group has prepared exhibits for kite museums in Japan and America.

'It's a unique tradition, bringing generations together,' says Ron Spaulding, a long-time expat and co-founder of the Thai Kite Heritage Group. 'What you see today at the King's Cup is the same as the people of Ayutthaya would have seen more than two hundred years ago.'

And what's the excitement all about? 'The action of a catch,' replies Spaulding. 'The pull down at break-neck speed and then quickly getting the kite back up again to bring down another victim, faster and faster. There's nothing like it. The battle of the sexes is, after all, timeless.'

THE
CHANGING WORLD

So rich and varied — and enduring — are facets of traditional Thai culture that any fascination with the contemporary pales in comparison. A sense of 'Thainess' is inevitably diminished in this age of multiculturalism and yet the local art scene and Bangkok itself display change and development that, while very modern, is also fundamentally and inimitably Thai.

CONTEMPORARY ART

Note: This article was written just before the economic crash of 1997 and since then the contemporary art scene has, to a degree, matured. Certainly, the economic meltdown prompted a younger generation of artists to both stylistic innovation and a greater breadth of vision, as well as a fresh commitment to political and social concerns. Sadly, Montien Boonma succumbed to cancer before fulfilling a career marked by extraordinary talent.

Thai art has come a long way in the 20th century. Exclusively religious in content and didactic in aim until the early 1900s, Thai painting was previously known, if at all, only for the traditional Buddhist temple murals. The country's first art school wasn't founded until the 1930s and only in recent decades have painters been able to survive as independent artists. Throwing off the shackles of repetitive mural art they have opened themselves up to a quest for a new aesthetic, not hidebound by parochial traditions yet still true to cultural roots.

Seeking a Thai mode of expression speaking an international language, artists have painted their way through the Western 'isms', from Impressionism to Post-modernism via Cubism and Surrealism. Many have now come full circle to reach Neo-traditionalism.

Such an eclectic probing of possibilities has, alas, produced little fruit. Thai artists now could well ponder the inscription of Gauguin's famous 1897 Tahitian painting: 'Where do we come from? What are we? Where are we going.' But, as Thailand's leading contemporary art curator, Dr Apinan Poshyananda, has half-jokingly remarked, the first two questions would likely have been considered irrelevant and the third is simply answered – 'where the money is'.

Ironically, while creativity is uncertain, the art scene booms and prices soar. There are more galleries in Bangkok now that at any other time and more exhibitions are being held in an ever-greater diversity of venues from the National Gallery to smart hotel lobbies. With prices starting at around the 25,000–50,000 baht mark, it is not unknown for even young art graduates to become baht millionaires after just one or two shows. Needless to say, prices bear little relationship to value and the boom belies problems that beset the Thai art scene.

The dilemma between valid contemporary forms and indigenous content is scarcely surprising when efforts have rarely gone beyond attempting to graft poorly-grasped Western styles on to a Thai cultural base. The beginnings of modern art in Thailand must be seen as inauspicious when Professor Silpa Bhirasri, founder of the nation's first fine arts school, now Silpakorn University, could defend poor imitations of Western models with such a weak argument as: 'The word "Impressionism" should not be understood as a copy of the Western Impressionist School ... impressionism means to express sincerely what we see and, accordingly, what we feel without any intellectual speculation.'

Alien influences are, however, inevitable when art today (and much else besides) is dominated by the West, not only styles and techniques which have been evolved in Europe or the US but also fundamental concepts of what art is or isn't and what the role of the artist should or shouldn't be. This is a fact, whether we like it or not and it is pointless to harp on about cultural colonialism. It is a meaningless phrase anyway when most modern development by and large follows Western patterns, rightly or wrongly. The trouble is that usually only the facile is adopted; underpinning concepts and values are commonly ignored.

Yet, cross-cultural exchanges can work. Such diverse influences as Japanese prints and African primitive art had an effective impact on European art in the late 19th and early 20th centuries. Conversely, much Japanese painting has evolved from long, if erratic, exposure to Western art.

It would be wrong, of course, to underestimate the profound differences in cultural assumptions that inhibit development in contemporary Thai art. Buddhism negates the notion of ego and views the material world as illusion, while in the West individual man, his qualities, struggles and achievements, are paramount. A further profound difference exists in Buddhism's unquestioning acceptance, compared to contemporary Western thought's tendency towards iconoclasm.

Compounding the difficulties posed by contrary philosophical assumptions in any cross-cultural exchange is the essential conservatism of Thai culture which functions by, among other things, non-confrontation, deference to superiors (judged by whatever yardstick) and an avoidance of criticism.

Thai art historian Dr Piriya Krairiksh makes a valid comment. 'One's standard is that Thai artists should be equal to the best internationally, that is what one hopes and aspires to. And if one isn't sincere in one's criticism, in saying the truth, nothing changes. In this culture people don't like to criticize, but unless there is constructive criticism one can never progress.'

If Herbert Read was correct in suggesting that art is subject, in so far as there is any observable law, 'to the law not of progress but of reaction', then development in Thai art is severely hampered by an historical lack of any critical tradition.

A non-critical stance, fuelled by conservatism and a rigid, status-obsessed social structure, leads to the death of the artist (commonly willingly accepted) as he or she is absorbed and neutered by a society bent on negating tensions and, ironically in view of its Buddhist base, materialistic in its outlook. So many artists of worth simply stop to all intents and purposes once they have achieved recognition. They appear content with a reputation and social standing, with the result that their work ceases to develop as the status and not the art becomes the object. At its most extreme this phenomenon manifests itself in painters producing the same picture over and over again. A case in point is Preecha Thaothong, whose studies of the effect of light and shade on classical mural and architectural forms have become tediously repetitive.

Even, or rather especially, Thawan Duchanee, Thailand's biggest name artist, appears to have fallen into this trap. Today, he is a star, darling of arty parties, loved for his outrageous acts and utterances because, safely pigeon-holed, he is like a tiger with its teeth pulled. That is a far cry from the early 1970s when one of his exhibitions so outraged some students that they destroyed paintings they considered sacrilegious.

Early on, Thawan arguably contributed the most in helping to put Thai contemporary art on a firmer footing. His concern and commitment to Buddhism, its philosophy, its concept of reality and its significance for man today were manifested as no simple handling of the surface gloss of Buddhist art. Rather he attempted to move away from clichés and portray and reinterpret the substance of Buddhist truth behind its symbols.

Displaying draughtsmanship of genius, Thawan's most typical works are convoluted, intensely detailed drawings, frequently depictions of either muscle-bound human forms or haunting, sometimes frightening, phantasmagorical animals. Western influences – notably elements derived from Hieronymous Bosch and figures from William Blake – can be discerned although they are in the main incorporated into a fresh expression of Buddhist concepts.

But perhaps the most original element in Thawan's work is its masculine quality, its sense of strength and power, raw guts as it were. This was something quite new for Thai art, which traditionally has been soft and decorative. Yet having introduced this potentially exciting element, the artist has subsequently done little to develop it. Thawan appears content with his fame – and fortune – and it is a moot point if he has produced anything worthy of his promise during the last decade.

Clearly, for art to benefit from cross-cultural variations – which equally clearly it must if it is to progress in an age of internationalism – the artist is faced with the enormous task of accommodating differing, if not always opposite, cultural and philosophical perspectives, as well as of defining and defending a role.

There are serious questions that need to be addressed if Thai art is to avoid superficiality, ponderous literalism and satisfaction with surface appearances. But the fact that they are not being adequately addressed points to a more fundamental malaise – complacency.

The current degree of corporate patronage and an emphasis on art as a commodity raising the financial stakes has prompted Dr Apinan to remark that 'pressing issues such as originality, identity, marginality and gender seem to take less priority among many Thai artists.' This results in their no longer caring 'if their products are criticized as stagnant and insipid as long as their goods have a market... Thai artists have quickly learnt that money has the power to turn kitsch into quality.'

With artists questing money instead of simply questing, few show any sustained development in their work. Such is the lack of individual progress that for many painters a retrospective exhibition would be meaningless.

There are however, a few artists who do endeavour to push their work forward, probe possibilities and resist complacency and a new generation of artists has moved Thai art along two distinct lines. One is neo-traditionalism, which builds on both the work of artists like Thawan and the older conventions of classical mural painting. The other is a more obviously modern approach employing multimedia and taking a less reverential stance towards established conventions.

Panya Vijinthanasarn is a notable example of the neo-traditionalist school. He attempts to give modern expression to classical mural forms and has over the past decade and more moved through phases, each distinct yet with a logical connection. From the montage works of his student days, through the hard-edge, nightmarish monsters of his paintings in the early 1980s to print-making during a spell at London's Slade School of Fine Arts and on to his more recent softer handling of classical motifs juxtaposed with contemporary images, he has experimented with various styles while preserving a consistency in his expressive concerns – 'a more intense expression of the same ideas that are found in traditional mural painting,' as he puts it.

Not totally free of succumbing to external pressures, Panya has on at least two occasions prostituted his work to paint murals for Thai pavilions at World Expos in Australia and Spain. Whether motivated by financial reasons, or through deference to the influential people who request his cooperation is irrelevant. Yet, the artist has retained his integrity. For example, at the same time as painting accomplished but essentially trite murals for Expo '92, Panya was producing experimental semi-abstract works by applying a hot iron to heat-sensitive paper with interesting results.

Development is integral to any assessment of Panya's achievement, indicative of his work as a whole, as well as being something that sets him apart from most of his contemporaries. He also maintains a healthy critical attitude. 'Artists in Thailand just try to do something like art,' he criticizes. 'They must be more serious. Art can be a pleasure but it is also something deeper. Most Thai artists think it is sufficient to be good in Thailand; that's not enough, we are international. I know I'm not as good as other artists outside; I have to try harder. The artist has to lead society, be beyond it, not working within in it... no stopping, always creating, moving... it's never the end.'

Neo-traditionalism has considerable expressive power, although it is inevitably limited in content and ideas. Not so the contemporary art of the likes of Montien Boonma, Vasan Sitthiket, Araya Rasjarmreansook, Navin Rawanchaikul and photographer Manit Sriwanichpoom. The work of these and other largely conceptual artists, who favour installations and other multimedia over conventional painting, addresses more 'difficult' subjects, such as anxiety, social alienation, consumerism, identity, gender and globalization.

This is perhaps the single most exciting aspect of today's Thai art scene – it is moving, questioning, exploring. The stylistic preoccupations represent a departure in a culture which has traditionally placed a premium on the decorative, valuing form over substance. A questioning attitude and a confirmed commitment to opening up new avenues of expression and giving greater relevancy to art and the role of the artist in society are what really distinguish this modern movement.

More satisfying than the variety of styles and modes of expression among this younger generation of painters is their creative drive and their refusal to be easily satisfied with monetary success. They are constantly challenging and provocative.

Paralleling the rapidity of social change in Thailand, Montien's output is prodigious, each exhibition showing something new, exciting and provocative. Through his installations and mixed-media works he is penetrating high technology while not abandoning Thai spiritualism. He is critical of trends in society, but, he insists, 'I never refute anything. I just ask how best to use it.'

In a word, Montien's art is about questioning and his essential integrity promises the emergence of a valid intellectual stance that rediscovers or reinforces essential values and concerns at a time when many in the Thai art world consider only market forces. 'I am not so much concerned with new style,' he says, 'but more about how I can transmit or express the images and ideas in my work... I never think my work should be more advanced than that of other artists. But I do think artists should know what is going on in the art world in particular and in the world in general.... at times I am actually more interested in the life of contemporary people than I am in the views of contemporary art.'

Panya and Montien are but two examples of artists who show

some commitment to improving an art scene troubled by a reluctance to address the important issues of identity, originality and social realities beyond the market-place. Only with the adoption of such a stance will the tensions arising from unavoidable, even desirable, cross-cultural pressures stand a chance of being resolved to produce an art which goes beyond the superficial, the literal and the downright bad.

BANGKOK REDEFINED

A metropolis in apparent transition, Bangkok saw out the 20th century with more physical change in less time than at any other period in its 200-year history. An unprecedented building boom reshaped the skyline in the late 1980s and early '90s; at the same time, the city was re-mapped by new multi-lane expressways, while in the last month of 1999 Bangkok celebrated the opening of its first rapid mass transit system. Then, as the year 2000 dawned, tunnellers were carving out a subway system, bringing to reality what had long been merely a pipedream of the more fanciful city planners. Bangkok's modern infrastructure development has been nothing short of breathtaking, probably unmatched in scale and speed by any other of the world's major cities.

When the Dusit Thani Hotel opened in 1970, it was Bangkok's tallest building, a status that went unchallenged until the 1980s. From its top-floor restaurant you could have looked down onto a traffic-clogged Rama IV Road and out beyond to uninterrupted birds' eye views of an urban pancake, a relentless concrete flatness stretching to a hazy horizon. By the end of the 1990s, the hotel had become dwarfed by new neighbours, lost in a forest of thrusting high-rises standing head and shoulders above it. Nor was it just buildings that had altered the location: the mid section of Rama IV Road had risen in a flyover, been crossed by the elevated track of a rapid mass transit system and undergone deep excavation for the construction of a subway station. None of this was exceptional and the changing face of this one tiny corner of Bangkok was reflected throughout the city.

Yet, while what is happening to Bangkok today in terms of its infrastructure undoubtedly represents one of the historic turning points in the city's evolution, there is an argument to be made that Bangkok never changes. This may seem absurd in view of the very obvious physical alteration, the shifting perspective in visual appearance encountered at every turn, but be that as it may, the Thai capital has always preserved a unique essence that keeps it, as Pico Iyer, the travel writer, has remarked, 'immutably and ineffably itself'. It certainly draws on alien influences in a highly eclectic fashion, although in adopting the 'other' it also adapts it and makes it its own.

By the start of the 20th century, Bangkok was beginning to assume its now familiar design. It is perhaps more accurate to say lack of design, since the city has no true downtown area and is more a collection of separate districts, each with its own ambience, that have merged to become a metropolis that is to a greater or lesser degree a definable entity.

Unplanned though development may have been, the growth of Bangkok over the last hundred years has been enormous, expanding from 13.2 square kilometres (5.1 sq. miles) in 1900 to a present-day greater metropolitan area of more than 330 sq. km (127 sq. miles). Increasingly, the Thai capital has been a city on the move, expanding urban areas into what were formerly paddy fields and moving upwards into the sky with high-rises.

The greatest acceleration came in the later years of the 20th century. In less than a generation the city transformed itself from an easy-going Asian capital into an energetic metropolis with a building boom beginning in the mid 1980s that changed Bangkok's appearance almost beyond recognition.

In the 1970s, Bangkok numbered fewer than 25 buildings taller than six storeys; by the end of the century there were close to 1,000 high-rises. Novelty in building volume was matched by novelty in architectural design. 'Sir,' wrote a reader to the *Bangkok Post* in the late 1980s, 'We have Ionic, Doric, Victorian, Mock Tudor, the glories of Mansard juxtaposed with pseudo Spanish and goodness knows what else. But now we have "Wizard of Id" Hollywood Gothic. What on earth is being taught to Thai architectural students?'

However, not all of Bangkok's buildings of the '80s and '90s succumbed to what has been described as the 'fruit salad style' of architecture. A graceful office tower such as Charn Issara, on Rama IV Road, showed simple yet pleasing lines. The angled glass curtain-walled offices of Thai Airways International were likewise attractive while successfully expressing a modern, thrusting spirit. Nor was all thought of cultural identity thrown to the wind, as illustrated by the Regent Bangkok (now The Four Seasons) hotel which in essence follows the traditional pattern of a group of Thai houses set around courtyards, gardens and watercourses.

Moreover, by the 1990s Bangkok had begun to embark on a more responsible phase of architectural development. Excesses declined and properties such as the superb Siam Commercial Bank headquarters on the northern outskirts of Bangkok showed that high-rises need not necessarily be boring glass boxes enlivened by Greek temple porticoes.

If modern Bangkok has become an architectural maze, the pathways through that maze, the city roads, are now far more ordered than in the past. For years, the Thai capital was notorious for its traffic jams and, in 1993, a team from the Massachusetts Institute of Technology (MIT) concluded that Bangkok had 'possibly the worst traffic congestion of any city of similar size in the world'.

Bangkok's biggest change in its 200-year history has been the switch from being a waterborne city, centred on the Chao Phraya river and its network of canals, to a road-based city in the manner of its US namesake, Los Angeles. Accordingly, Bangkok has become a car-crazy city with less than 9% of its land area taken up by roads, compared to the norm of 20%–25%.

In spite of the growth of Bangkok as a city increasingly dominated by the automobile – whose numbers totalled more than 3 million and rising in 1999 – there was little public investment in major roads until the 1980s.

Positive gains were few until a two-stage system of elevated expressways was constructed to provide lanes for through-traffic on levels above the general roads. The 27.1-km (16¾-mile) first stage, with its main sections linking the port at Klong Toey to Dindaeng in the north of the city and to Bangna in the east, was completed in the early 1980s. A third section to Dao Kanong was opened in 1987.

These links were significantly extended in the 1990s by the complementary systems of an elevated tollway to Don Muang Airport, while in the year 2000 a 55-km (34-mile) elevated road from Bangna to the Eastern Seaboard was completed. Improving the situation further was a second-stage elevated expressway, operated by a concessionaire and consisting of a 32-km (20-mile) north-south link, also completed in the 1990s.

Initially, traffic was as clogged on the first-stage expressway as it was on the streets and cynics dubbed the system 'an elevated parking lot'. But once all the links were in place, the combined system dramatically improved traffic flow through and around the city.

Pandering to the automobile, however, is not everything and December 1999 represented a milestone for Bangkok; no longer would the city have the dubious distinction of being one of the few major world capitals without a mass transit system of any kind. The inauguration of the Skytrain in that month finally ended four decades of debate, promises and delays and at last Bangkok had at least the beginnings of what it needs to survive as a modern metropolis.

Linking key destinations on a 23.5-kilometre (14½-mile) route around town, the Skytrain travels at an average speed of 35 kph (21 mph) – at least three times the usual pace of cars in central Bangkok. A 17-kilometre (10½-mile) cross-town journey, for example, from the popular Chatuchak Market to Sukhumvit Soi 81 in Phrakanong, can now be completed in less than 30 minutes, compared to the frustrating 90 minutes or more it can take by car.

The system has its critics, voicing concern that it had been planned without due regard to the environment and aesthetics, but an overall assessment shows greater gain than loss. The arguments of the detractors are debatable and while certain black-spots – stations such as Saladaeng on Silom Road – that do turn the streets below into 150 metre- (492-foot) long tunnels that darken the sidewalks and trap traffic fumes, the environmental aspects of the Skytrain, given its necessity, are generally more positive than negative.

As for aesthetics, the challenge of how to give a million tons of concrete and steel an acceptable appearance was remarkably well met. Aside from a few awkward areas, the massive system is not the eyesore it could so easily have been. For the most part, the elegantly designed support columns and the graceful curves of the viaduct add interesting patterns to the city's modern mosaic.

As people become used to the Skytrain, it emphatically alters the way in which they experience Bangkok. It is as if time and space in the city have become new dimensions. Also, the city is viewed differently. Seen from the vantage point of 12 metres (40 feet) above the streets, Bangkok reveals itself as a far greener city than imagined with gardens normally hidden behind compound walls suddenly exposed. Landmarks, too, are seen afresh. Victory Monument, for example, was previously lost amid the chaos of a major traffic intersection. Now as the Skytrain glides by in a graceful sweep, the needle spire and flanking statuary appear larger and more imposing than before.

Yet the most striking thing about the Skytrain is that it is novel. It is not merely new; it is radically different from anything the city has previously known. With its computerized systems it brings a sense of order to cross-town travel. It is also clean, cool and quiet – further elements previously conspicuously absent when travelling around the city.

Now, with the Skytrain completed, Bangkok enters the 21st century in the throes of building another massive infrastructure project, a subway system covering a 20-kilometre (12½-mile) route from Hua Lamphong to Bang Sue with 18 stations and due for completion in 2003. Given that the Thai capital, built on an alluvial plain, is prone to flooding, the very idea of a subway is surprising. However, using the same technique and technology as were employed in the construction of the Channel Tunnel that links Britain and France, Bangkok's subway is a viable proposition. Even so, as a precaution, station entrances have been built one metre (3¼ feet) above the highest flood level recorded over the past 200 years.

The excavation of the tunnel itself, at an average depth of 23 metres (75 feet) below the city streets and with a finished internal diameter of 5.7 metres (18¾ feet), is a marvel of modern technology, employing the 'Earth Pressure Balance Shield' system in which the tunnel is bored and walled in one operation. The nuts and bolts of this system is a bullet-shaped machine with a blunt nose to which is fixed a rotating cutter rather like a propeller with teeth.

Having to cope mainly with only the clay on which Bangkok sits, tunnelling progresses at a rate of one centimetre (a third of an inch) a minute. With added time for installation of the tunnel walls and removal of the excavated earth, Bangkok's subway is advancing at an average pace of 10 metres (33 feet) a day. When completed it is expected that some 400,000 commuters a day will be travelling underground.

So, where is Bangkok today? Arguably, it has never been better in modern times; it is greener than before, traffic flow is showing marked improvement and a greater sense of order is being brought to the previous near chaos. At the same time, a 'Thainess' of character and image survives, albeit tenuously balanced, to keep Bangkok uniquely itself as it continues to develop and change.

SUGGESTED FURTHER READING

Boisselier, Jean, *The Heritage of Thai Sculpture* (Bangkok, Asia Books, 1975)

Boisselier, Jean, *Thai Painting* (Tokyo, Kodansha International, 1976)

Bowers, Faubion, *Theatre in the East* (New York, Thomas Nelson & Sons, 1956)

Bowring, Sir John, *The Kingdom and People of Siam* (2 vols, reprint, Kuala Lumpur, Oxford University Press, 1969)

Clutterbuck, Martin R., *The Legend of Siamese Cats* (Bangkok, White Lotus, 1998)

Gervaise, Nicolas, *The Natural and Political History of The Kingdom of Siam* (reprint Bangkok, White Lotus, 1989)

Ginsburg, Henry, *Thai Manuscript Painting* (Honolulu, University of Hawaii Press, 1989)

Gorer, Geoffrey, *Bali and Angkor* (London, Michael Joseph, 1936)

Graham, W.A., *Siam* (2 vols, London, Alexander Moring, 1924)

Guelden, Marlane, *Thailand: Into the Spirit World* (Singapore, Times Editions, 1995)

Hoskin, John, *Ten Contemporary Thai Artists* (Bangkok, Graphis, 1984)

Loubère, Simon de la, *The Kingdom of Siam* (reprint, Bangkok, White Lotus, 1986)

Maugham, Somerset, *The Gentleman in the Parlour* (London, Heinemann, 1930)

Nithi, Sthapitanonda and Mertens, Brian, *Architecture of Thailand* (Bangkok, Asia Books, 2005)

Plamintr, Sunthorn, *Getting To Know Buddhism* (Bangkok, Buddhadhamma Foundation, 1994)

Poshyananda, Apinan, *Modern Art in Thailand* (Singapore, Oxford University Press, 1992)

Rutnin, Mattani (ed), *The Siamese Theatre* (Bangkok, The Siam Society, 1975)

Tachard, Guy, *Voyage to Siam* (reprint, Bangkok, White Orchid Press, 1981)

Terwiel, B.J., *Monks and Magic* (Bangkok, White Lotus, 1994)

Thongthep, Meechai (compiler), *Ramakien: The Thai Ramayana*, (Bangkok, Naga Books, 1993)

Tonkin, Derek, *Simple Etiquette in Thailand* (Sandgate, Paul Norbury Publications, 1990)

Van Beek, Steve and Tettoni, Luca Invernizzi, *The Arts of Thailand* (Hong Kong, Travel Publishing Asia, 1985)

Wyatt, David K, *Thailand: A Short History* (London, Yale University Press, 1984)

INDEX